D0717723

8/92

# A HERITAGE AND ITS HISTORY

# A HERITAGE AND ITS HISTORY

by

## I. COMPTON-BURNETT

LONDON
VICTOR GOLLANCZ LTD
1979

© I. Compton-Burnett 1959

First published 1959
Reissued 1979

ISBN 0 575 02723 1

*Printed in Great Britain at
The Camelot Press Ltd, Southampton*

# A HERITAGE AND ITS HISTORY

# CHAPTER I

"It is a pity you have not my charm, Simon," said Walter Challoner.

"Well, we hardly want a double share in a family."

"I am glad you are all without it. It is untrue that we cannot have too much of a good thing. I could not bear to be one amongst many. It would not suit the something there is about me."

"I don't see anything to mind in it."

"But is there anything about you, Simon?"

"It would not help me if there was. One amongst many is what I am. The number of us is my trouble. My uncle has his dealings with my father, and my father passes them on to me. I have no personal scope. My youth is escaping without giving me anything it owes me. I see it shortening before my eyes. And Uncle must leave everything to Father, before I even become the heir. It throws my life into an indefinite future. I never put it into words, but I carry a burden about with me."

"It is praiseworthy not to put it into words. I wonder how it would be, if you did."

"Words do not hasten things," said Simon.

"No, or yours would have done so. Can it be that you have death in your heart? What a different thing from charm! To think of the gulf between us! I wonder if there is any outward sign of it."

The brothers did present a difference, as they stood in the family dining-room. Walter was short and pale and spare, with long, narrow features and alert, light eyes, and sudden, uneven movements that seemed to be a part of him. Simon, three years older, and now a man of twenty-five, was tall and large and heavily made, with a florid,

7

regular face, lively, brown eyes, and the precise and easy movements that tend to go with weight. Something in the firm profile and supple hands of both suggested the tie of blood.

"Well, charm should be on the surface," said Simon. "It has no hidden use."

"It does what it can, one poor little portion amongst all that is without it. Strive on, Walter Challoner, and the charm you see in secret, you can reward openly."

"There is none in being blasphemous," said Simon, looking at the breakfast table.

"Simon, surely you are a modern man."

"And none in ignoring conventions. And real charm should be unconscious."

"No good quality is that. Good qualities involve effort. Without it they would not exist. Think of charity and tolerance. Even with it they exist uncertainly. But charm is perhaps more of the nature of a gift. It makes me humble as well as proud."

"I can only be the first. I have no chance of being what I might. I serve the place through other men, and feel my own powers wasted."

"It is pleasant to be conscious of powers. I admit I find it so. And they ought to have their outlet. But your heart is unduly set on the place. It seems to be the meaning of your life."

"I do not deny it or wish it. I love it as I could never love anything else. Even you are second to it. Wife and child could never be more to me. I shall need them, in order to hand it on to my descendants. That will be their first meaning. And my hands are tied. I can order and alter nothing. You are in a better position, pretending to be a poet."

"Simon, pray do not talk to me like a member of my family. And just as you were being so different! I seldom speak of my ambitions or their fate. There is a good deal of quiet courage in my life. Turn your eyes on it, and let it lead you onward."

8

"That is the last thing I can hope for. I am held back in everything. Look at this room and its dinginess! It gets darker with every day. It is that creeper smothering the house. And I can do nothing. When the place is mine, I shall have it cut away."

"I did not mean you to be led as far onward as that. Uncle Edwin and Father would both have to die."

"Well, people must die in the end."

"Of course they must not. People are immortal. You must have noticed it. Indeed you betray that you have."

"I wish I could think I was. My time will be too short to serve any purpose. And there are things I want to do so much."

"Your voice broke with pardonable emotion. I had not met that before. So it is true that books are based on life. But you plan to do things when two people are dead. That proves you are immortal. It is they who are not."

"It is what they seem to be. And older people would naturally die first."

"Well, Nature is cruel. We are told about it. They ought to have the first claims. They are led to expect them."

"Who is cruel?" said another voice, as an elderly man entered the room. "Good-morning to you both."

"Good-morning, Uncle," said the two young men together.

"Nature is cruel," said Walter. "She lets older people die before young, when they have a better right to live, as they have that to everything."

"And have formed the habit of living," said Simon, easily.

"Yes," said Sir Edwin, glancing at him. "But people may not die in order of age."

"What did I tell you?" murmured Walter. "You see he is immortal. Or anyhow he sees it."

"What made you think about death? It is a thought for my age rather than yours."

"The creeper on the house," said Simon. "It has had its time."

9

"So have many of us. But I hope it is not dying? I planted it myself fifty years ago. And I feel that gives it a claim on life. I cannot give a reason."

"I cannot either," said Simon, laughing.

"I can," murmured Walter. "It helps him to feel there is no such thing as death. If it dies, he will see there is.—No, it is not dying, Uncle. But Simon wishes it was. He says it darkens the house."

"It may do so. I daresay I do the same. It is a thing that comes with age. But it will be left as it is, as I shall be. We will be allowed to grow old together."

"What do you mean, Uncle? You know you are our sunshine."

Sir Edwin laughed, but looked at his elder nephew.

"He was saying he would have it cut down, when the place was his? No, I was not listening at the door. He need not admit it."

"Uncle, are you trying to introduce an element of discomfort?"

"That tends to come, when death is mentioned, and someone over sixty is in the room."

"Sixty!" murmured Walter. "When he is sixty-nine! He does mean to be immortal."

"Good-morning to you all," said another voice. "Here is someone else over sixty. It is a common thing. What is the talk about it?"

"Not as common as being in the twenties," said Sir Edwin, "nor held to be."

"But quite ordinary," said Walter. "That is what I really think. It is the secret of my appeal."

"If it is a secret, why not keep it?" said Simon.

"It seems to need explanation. Charm is so elusive."

"Well, we have had our help," said his uncle.

The elder pair of brothers made as great a contrast as the younger, and seemed to combine their attributes with their own. Sir Edwin had Simon's height and Walter's spareness and pallor, a fuller brow than either, and deep, grey eyes, with a piercing quality they seemed to try to veil. His brother was as short as his second son, and as dark as the first, with firm, sunken features and sunken, sombre eyes, and a suggestion about him of a failing hold on life. All four had the straightness of bone and suppleness of hand that went to the family type.

"Your young men talk of demolishing the creeper on the house, Hamish," said Sir Edwin. "It is encroaching, as old things do. They must accept our sympathy with it."

"I remember your planting it. We have gone through the years together. And changed with them, as we must. And it has no designs on our lives."

"I am not so sure," said Simon, laughing. "It takes your light for itself."

"And stands in yours in a way," said Sir Edwin. "Or is involved with those who do."

"I meant just what I said, Uncle. It is not good to live in shade. You would be better with it gone."

"We are clinging to life. I think you would not deny it."

"It is the fault of the old, that they do that," said Hamish.

"You both seem to think you are a hundred," said Walter.

"No, I hardly like to think I am sixty-nine, as you have observed," said Sir Edwin.

"You ought to be just a little deaf, Uncle."

"We are not always treated as what we ought to be. I think we seldom are. Perhaps I am fortunate."

"Uncle, pray do not speak to me in a dry manner."

"We don't know how long the creeper lives," said Simon.

"Something else we have in common with it," said his father.

"It used to be forbidden to talk about age," said Sir Edwin. "When a custom is broken, we see what lies at the back of it. There is reason behind all convention."

"I think we may talk about the age of a plant," said Simon.

"This plant is nothing to do with you or me," said Hamish, gently. "The house and what is in or on it are your uncle's."

"They are for the time. But they are to do with all of us. Each of us in turn holds them in trust."

"But not out of his turn," said Sir Edwin. "We live in the present, not in the ultimate future. We need not voice our thoughts about it."

"Ultimate future!" murmured Walter. "Indeed they are immortal."

"We are, or ought to be, as far as your brother is concerned. Looking past other people's lives is a poor habit."

"What habit is that?" said another voice, as a grey-haired woman entered the room. "Simon, you are not beginning the day by arguing with your uncle?"

"I am glad to hear it," said her son. "I was afraid I was."

"I quarrel with anyone who peoples his world simply with himself," said Sir Edwin.

"Some people must see themselves in their place," said Hamish. "Simon's is not his fault. He cannot help knowing it."

"He talks as if he had no other interest."

"Well, what other has he, Edwin?" said Mrs. Challoner. "We have not so much in our life."

"People should wait for changes to come. And they may safely do so."

"Who brought up the subject? It is not a good one for the morning."

"The creeper on the house, Mater," said Simon. "I said it should be cut down."

"And implied that it would be," said Hamish. "And we throw no doubt on it. But everything has its time."

"We know not on what day nor at what hour——" said his wife. "But what is wrong with the creeper? It adds so much to the house."

"Too much," said Simon. "It throws its shadow all

over it. This room is like a dungeon. I should be thankful to see it gone."

"I should be most distressed. It is a part of my home to me, of the background cf my married life. It will not go with my consent."

"Then it will not go," said her son.

"Has the creeper a name?" said Walter.

"No one knows it," said Simon. "And no one has taken the trouble to find out. And the name we give it suits it, the thing that creeps."

Julia Challoner was a long-limbed, upright woman of fifty-eight, with clear, hazel eyes, waving, grey hair, hands that might have met a demand, if one had been made, and a face that was at once roughly-hewn and handsome, pleasant and prone to cloud. She and her husband had lost their early feeling, but retained dependence and trust; and of late her affection for him had been charged with her fears for his health. She was both critical and fond as a mother, and would have found more fault than she did, had not a natural, nervous discontent been held in check by her religion.

"Do you know the name of the creeper on the house, Deakin?" she said, as the butler entered.

The latter mentioned two Latin words in an even tone.

"What is the popular name?" said Simon.

"I am not aware of that, sir."

"Neither am I," said Walter. "And I find I am proud of it."

"Could not the gardener tell us?" said Hamish.

"He does not make use of popular names, sir."

"So I am equal to him," said Walter.

"What do you feel about the creeper itself, Deakin?" said Julia. "You would not like to see it go?"

"Well, ma'am, it would be a piece of life gone. But we are used to yielding it, little by little."

"I never become so," said Hamish. "Not even as I yield it more fully. I am always surprised by the lowering cloud."

"And we cannot depend on the silver lining, sir," said Deakin. "I have seen many clouds without it."

"I have never seen one with it," said Walter. "My clouds have been so very black."

"Well, the lighter the lining, sir, the darker the cloud may seem."

"You pride yourself on pessimism, Deakin," said Julia.

"Well, ma'am, when we are told to look on the bright side of things, it is not generally at a happy time."

"But it is good advice for daily life."

"Daily life harbours everything, ma'am. All our troubles come into it."

"You are a subtle talker, Deakin," said Walter.

"Well, sir, there may be a tendency. And I have had examples."

"I could never copy anyone," said Simon.

"I think that is true," said his father.

"Copy was not a term I employed, sir," said Deakin.

"Father said a generous word to you, Simon," said Walter.

"Well, I am content with my own level. And I am sure Deakin is with his."

"Well, sir, if we had the choice of position, it might not have fallen on mine. Indeed we might say it would not. But I do not quarrel with fate. It is not a contest in which we should emerge victorious."

"I meant you were content with your personal standard."

"Well, sir, it is hardly for me to comment there."

"I wonder how many of us are dissatisfied with it," said Hamish.

"Very few of us," said Julia. "We like to be ourselves. And often it is what other people like us to be."

"Yes, for many reasons," said Walter.

"They may not welcome encroachment, sir," said Deakin, almost with a smile.

"We have forgotten about the creeper," said Simon.

"I think not," said Sir Edwin. "Anyhow you have remembered it. But it might be as well forgotten."

Deakin was an angular, middle-aged man, with pale, hollow eyes and a hollow-cheeked face, whose look of complete resignation was the key to his nature. He had been for years with the family, and had as high an opinion of it, as it was in him to hold. He had a peculiar regard for Julia, whose aloofness from household matters he approved; and much that might have been her province, he attended to himself, without intensifying his demeanour. He looked at her now with a sympathetic eye, as she addressed her younger son, feeling that in any difference right would be on her side.

"When are you returning to Oxford, Walter?"

"I am not doing so, Mater."

"What do you mean? The term must almost have begun."

"It has done so. Simon will tell you about it. I am too tender a plant for such a harsh wind."

"He has been expelled," said Simon, in his easy manner.

"Oh, I have not. You should temper the wind to us. It was intimated that I should not return, as the life was not suited to me. Deakin looks as if he understands."

"Life is not exactly adapted to any of us, sir. The conforming is not on that side."

"That is what you did not realise, Walter," said Julia.

"I could not conform, Mater. I am not on the usual line. You would not wish to have an average son."

"Tell us about it fully," said Hamish.

"Father, do not speak to me in short, terse tones. Remember that I owe you my being. And all is told."

"Why did your tutor not write to us?" said Sir Edwin.

"Because I begged him not to. I mean I forbade him to. And the course was nearly at an end."

"Surely you could have finished it, and taken your degree," said Julia. "What was the object of your being there?"

"I have never known, Mater. But I could not be examined. The very word seemed to degrade."

"Examiners are not inquisitors," said Sir Edwin.

"What makes you say that, Uncle?"

"I hardly see a reason," said Hamish, smiling.

"I hope you are really ashamed of yourself," said Julia.

"I am ashamed of my position, Mater. It is most embarrassing. If my shame communicates itself to you, we will suffer it together. What does Deakin feel about it?"

"We have to render what is required of us, sir," said the latter, continuing his duties.

"How did you spend your time at Oxford?" said Hamish, in simple question.

"I wrote poems, Father."

"Amongst other things?"

"No, I just wrote poems. What do you imply? Of course I am not a wild young man."

"Were the poems good ones?"

"Yes, but not so good, when I went back to them. And I had the courage to recognise it."

"And so you destroyed them?"

"Father, they are easy words. Few people have the strength to reject their early efforts."

"There must be many instances of it," said Julia. "There can be no record."

"It probably means you are a critic and not a poet," said Sir Edwin.

"Does it, Uncle? It is a terrible meaning. But I am pleased that you can talk to me in respectful terms."

"We are not proud of you, Walter," said Julia.

"I thought mothers were proud of their sons in spite of everything."

"Poetry will not take you far in life. Anyhow it will not support you."

"What I shall have, will be enough for me. I ask but little."

"What will happen, if you marry?"

"Disaster. But I shall not do so."

"You cannot know at your age."

"He does know," said Hamish. "It is like the poems. He may find later that it is different. But I am not sure."

"Did you ever write poems yourself, Father?" said Walter, looking at him.

"Yes, good ones, as you have, and then showed the same courage. It must run in the family. As your mother says, it may be in many."

"And you see yourself as a critic and not a poet," said Sir Edwin.

"What you said to me," said Walter. "I do like it to be the same."

"Well, we are most of us critics of many things," said Hamish, putting the matter more generally.

Deakin raised his shoulders with a faint smile, as though feeling this unavoidable.

"I am a critic of Walter's poems," said Simon, lightly.

"And you feel it exalts you," said his brother. "But if that is what you want, you should be the first to recognise them."

"That position is occupied," said Simon, with a laugh.

"It is better to be generous than to be gifted," said Julia.

"But it is not so congenial," said Hamish. "The generous person has to give more admiration than he feels. And he has such a different sort himself."

"A terrible sort," said Walter.

"Well, I shall not have any," said Simon.

"You will have another kind," said Walter. "You will be esteemed for your place."

"It seems to be honest esteem," said Hamish. "Well, I suppose we are to humour you, Walter."

"Well, I should like it, Father."

"There is something I should not disguise from you," said Sir Edwin. "Your father's health makes him reluctant to fail you at this time."

"It somehow seems better to disguise it," said Hamish.

"I shall be happy to have both my sons at home," said Julia. "But I am not sure how to take the good fortune."

"You and I will share it, Mater," said Walter. "And we will not forget that Simon is one of us."

"I am not afraid of your feeling for each other."

"Simon, do you feel you deserve this?"

"Do you expect to earn anything by your poems?" said Sir Edwin.

"Well, Uncle, I do imagine it."

"Poets may live in the world of imagination," said Hamish.

"Destroying the poems is not the way to earn by them," said Julia.

"Isn't it, Mater? It is supposed to be in the end."

"I hope you have no bills from Oxford?" said Sir Edwin.

"No, none, Uncle. I destroyed them with the poems."

"All that pile that I saw?" said Simon.

"The bills," said Walter. "The poems were not a pile. Or not those I destroyed."

"Did you destroy the bills without paying them?" said Julia.

"If I had paid them, they would not be bills, Mater. They would be receipts. And I put those in a drawer."

"You are very boyish, Walter."

"Mater, if you meant to wound me, you have done so. But it is a sad kind of success."

"They will come in again," said Julia.

"So they will. So my destroying them does not matter."

"You will not ask your mother to pay them," said Sir Edwin.

"Indeed no, Uncle. Of course we do not ask."

"The tradesmen have to live," said Julia. "Did you think of that?"

"No, but I found they did. They told me about it. And if they die, the bills come in. They live on in them."

"They are trifling bills," said Simon. "Mine were much larger. Uncle Edwin paid them."

"Your position is different," said his mother.

"So it is," said Walter. "And I have never had a grudging thought."

"Perhaps it is fair that you should live in your own way.

It is a freedom Simon will not have. It may be worth while to make sacrifices for it."

"It is a good thing Mater feels that, as she is to make them," said Simon.

"Mater, how deeply you speak!" said Walter.

"Well, I am not a stupid woman. It may be from me that you inherit your gifts. Talented men often have remarkable mothers."

"So we know where to place you both," said Sir Edwin.

"Uncle, those words were better not said. You should not speak with an ironic note."

"Is there any way in which we may speak?"

"Very few ways. Most of them shock me so much."

"Are we to remain at the breakfast table until luncheon is put upon it?"

"It would save our coming back for it," said Simon.

"I should require time for the adjustment, sir," said Deakin, without raising his eyes.

"Ought you not to be finding something to do?" said Julia, to her sons.

"Simon will not find that hard," said Hamish. "I am no longer equal to much. And Edwin wants him to get an insight into things. The future must be remembered."

"And we have seen that he does not forget it," said Sir Edwin.

"How do you feel this morning, Father?" said Simon, in a tone of concern.

"I feel no difference day by day. It is every month or so that I know a change. When a heart begins to go downhill, it knows no turning."

"I shall talk like that one day," said Walter. "I like to imagine it. It puts people in a very becoming light."

"In what way?" said his father.

"It shows them as dignified and courageous and not over-regardful of self. And what could be better?"

"To be quite unregardful of it, I suppose. But a bodily state may prevent it."

Julia leaned forward and put her hand on her husband's. She loved him less than she loved her sons, but wished to be and to seem a devoted wife. He accepted what she gave, knowing she gave what she could, knowing he gave no more. His brother had always been the centre of his life.

He waited for Julia and her sons to withdraw, and then turned to Sir Edwin.

"How poor a thing human feeling seems, to anyone forced to test it! And how strong the love of the things that last our life! I feel I have only just known it."

"We have had our help to-day."

"Well, nothing can last any longer. It is natural to want them at their time. My boy is more open than many people. He shows the feelings they try to hide. It may not prove they are so deep."

"It shows that he is not. And we must take him as he is, as people say. As if we had the choice!"

"Though my life is ending, yours is not. The future is in no one's hands. And he imagines it in his."

"Yes, for him his place is not the best."

"It is the one he would choose, the one you would have chosen. You have never regretted having it. We talk of its snares, but other lives have them. And they are met more often."

"Walter thinks he will avoid them. I suppose you must let him choose his path?"

"We should be glad he has made a choice. We cannot give him many. We must accept the difference in the lives of my sons, as they accept it."

"I hope their friendship will stand it, as ours has done. Having that, they cannot have nothing. We have not had it. But would your wife have done better in a life that asked more of her?"

"None of us escapes demands. She has not done so. She would hardly wish she had had more. We need not wish it for her. I am not in a mood to exalt demands. My last and longest is upon me."

"And upon me too. I am to live without you, Hamish, in a sense to die alone. No one will meet it with me. There the fault may be yours and mine. I shall carry you with me, consult you in the questions that arise. I know you enough to know what you would say. I shall say it to myself for you. But the silence of your voice will be silence for me. It is a thing that you will not suffer. Is that someone outside the door? Are your two lads listening?"

"If so, they have gained little. And nothing that would serve them."

"Their concern is not the end of our lives, but the beginning of their own. Though Walter may have thought we were occupied with his failings."

Walter had feared this, and had taken a position that would enlighten him. As his brother passed with a smile of connivance, he beckoned him to his side.

"Are they talking of you?" said Simon.

"No, of themselves. It is strange that I was not in their thoughts."

"What were they saying?"

"Noble things to each other about life and death. I wish I had not listened. I really had a right to hear no good of myself. And I heard so much good of them, that I shall never be at ease with them again."

"Did you not hear anything of us?"

"Only words of gentle acceptance of what we are. And I did not know they knew. They see us with open eyes, as we see them. And that is a shock."

"We don't seem to have seen the whole of them."

"Well, I have seen it now. Or I hope it is the whole. I hardly think there can be any more."

"Anyhow we will not find it out," said Simon.

"And I was confused by their not talking about my debts. I did not think of other things being in their thoughts. It might almost seem that my being in debt did not matter."

"Or that you did not," said Simon, laughing. "So they did not mention them?"

"Well, they heard me outside the door and guessed I thought they would be doing so. And they were not, which was humbling for me. I could rise above that, but they knew it was humbling; and from that I turn my eyes."

"You might have got more into debt, if you had known."

"Or I might not have done so at all. I did not know it was not a serious thing."

"Well, it is not, compared to Father's health. They must think first of that."

"That will do, Simon. I am brought low."

"It is not a good prospect for either."

"I wish it did not bring out the best in them. The best in people causes me such discomfort. And I hardly think it does much for anyone. It is difficult to see what good it is."

"I daresay you would not mind it in yourself."

"There is none in me," said Walter. "When I tried to find some to correspond with theirs, I found nothing but natural, human feelings."

"Perhaps you are none the worse for that."

"Yes, I am much worse."

"I suppose our friendship is an echo of theirs to them. And they hope it will serve us as well."

"It would have been no good for you to listen. You may be more like them than they know."

"They certainly do not know," said Simon, laughing.

"Ought we to promise faithfulness, as Uncle did?"

"I promise it," said Simon.

"So do I. So now we are equal to them, though they do not suspect it. Perhaps it adds to us to be a little misunderstood."

"It is a pity they don't know they are adding to us, when they would think it so desirable."

"Simon, I did like the serious note underlying your promise. Perhaps we are more than equal to them."

"To your father and uncle?" said Julia, passing through the hall. "You can only do your best to reach their level."

"We have reached it," said Walter. "You were not in time to hear."

"Walter, our lenience about your debts does not mean we are not troubled by them."

"No, Mater, of course it makes me regret them more."

"And you need not regard me as too simple a person."

"How could I, when it is known that sons take after their mothers?"

"You will turn over a new leaf, like my good son," said Julia, as she went her way.

"Yes, I hope you will do so, Walter," said Sir Edwin, coming out of the dining-room. "We do not talk of your troubles——"

"I know you do not, Uncle."

"As things are, they will be your affair more than ours."

"I wish people *would* talk of Walter's troubles," said Simon. "When they don't, they seem a recurring topic."

"One more word, Walter. I need only say it once. You are old to listen at doors."

"I don't think I am old enough, Uncle. For contact with the depths of life."

"Neither is anyone," said Hamish. "I try to forget I am involved in them. You must do the same."

"I think they have done so," said Sir Edwin. "They must expect us sometimes to remember."

Walter looked after the older men.

"It is terrible to meet selfless courage and try to be worthy of such a father. And in a way it is easier for him. He only has to feel that his sons are not equal to him. And there may be a shred of comfort there."

"I don't think we are less intelligent than he is."

"Simon, pride of intellect is not in place."

"Very few things are. And being in debt is hardly one of them. Of course I am not talking of your troubles."

"I shall have to remain in it. I cannot ask Father about such things, when he is on the brink of eternity."

"Put the bills on Mater's table. I daresay she will pay them. She likes to be trusted."

23

"I am glad to cause her pleasure. I will give her my full trust."

"Do you really think that Father will live to eternity?"

"Of course I do not. I should be as ashamed of it, as you would. I meant an eternity of nothingness, which was a good thing to mean. It almost seems you might mean something else. I admire Father for quietly facing extinction. I see nothing in facing eternity, when we should all like to so much."

"What does Father think himself?" said Simon.

"He thinks what we do, and knows we think it. It makes it hard to know how to behave with him."

"He said we were to forget it. I suppose he meant what he said."

"Simon, how can you suppose that?"

"If he heard us talking, what would he think?"

"That we were covering our feelings. Or I hope he would. And in my case there would be truth in it. In yours there is the knowledge that there will be a person less in your path."

"I do not really consider that. If I did, I should not talk of it. And it will not be so much of a change for me. I have seen Uncle's life as a better one than Father's. And a feeling is not less strong, that another can exist with it."

"I think the strife between them weakens it, when it is not strong enough to kill the other."

"You need not be so sure you are nobler than I am."

"I am sure," said Walter.

"You are giving Father more worry."

"Well, the black sheep does turn out to have the deepest heart."

"Now Deakin wants you out of the way," said Julia, returning to the hall. "He has to attend to his work. And, Simon, you should do the same. The day will be gone before you have begun."

"I thought I felt it going," said Walter. "There was less of the bleakness of having the whole morning before me."

"It can be a trying position, Deakin, to be the one woman in a family."

"I have thought it at times, ma'am. There is the lack of interchange. Not that there is ever that, except in a measure."

"I suppose your problem is the opposite, in your life in a group of women."

"Well, ma'am, life! I move and breathe among them."

"We have found you a good friend. This anxiety about Mr. Hamish is yours as well as ours."

"Yes, ma'am, it adds a touch of darkness to the greyness of life. And may perhaps help us to see it as no more than grey."

"You feel things are as gloomy as that?"

"There seems no reason for denying it, ma'am."

"I hope you are happy with us?"

"Yes, ma'am, as the word is used."

"I have had a good deal of joy in my life."

"It is looking back, ma'am. Distance lends what is needed. Though I would hardly employ the usual term."

"Have you no happy memories?"

"Well, they are uniform, ma'am."

"Perhaps your life has been more monotonous than mine."

"Well, ma'am, neither has left its groove."

"You have the satisfaction of feeling useful years behind you."

"And also before me, ma'am. And there are other epithets."

"I do not think lives lived solely for ourselves are any happier."

"Well, ma'am, few have the experience."

"The friendship between Sir Edwin and Mr. Hamish has done much for them."

"Yes, ma'am, it has come to their help."

"I hope my sons' friendship will serve them as well."

"Yes, ma'am. It is all before them."

"The stress of life?"

"Well, ma'am, its negation."

"Perhaps you should have married, Deakin."

"No, ma'am. There is no end but one."

"You know I do not see it as the end."

"No, you are prepared to go on, ma'am."

"Do you not feel it is a happier belief?"

"That hardly bears on it, ma'am. Choice does not play much part."

"So you do not look beyond your death?"

"I have imagined feeling it was all over at last, ma'am. It would seem a sort of compensation. But that is not a thing to expect."

# CHAPTER II

"THERE IS NO reason for being as late as this," said Fanny Graham to her sister.

"We do not know yet. There may be many."

"Well, there may be one."

"Then we will wait to judge."

"My judgement is ready. I don't feel it will be wasted."

"Why judge at all?" said Rhoda. "It is not one of our duties to each other."

"It seems it must be. Unless it is a duty to ourselves."

"We ourselves may sometimes be wrong."

"Well, then we are said to be."

"We can find other people as little wrong as possible."

"I find them as wrong as they are."

"It may be difficult to judge of that."

"Can it be? Everyone finds it so easy."

"There is no need to voice our judgements."

"Silent ones are said to do more. And if we are never to blame anyone, what of the people who deserve praise?"

"It is true they do not have it very often."

"Well, I think they deserve blame more."

"Do you feel that of yourself?"

"Well, I am better than most people. Are not you?"

"Now let me think about that," said Rhoda, leaning back. "You mean in my own opinion?"

"You would not be better in other people's. Or they could not be."

"There are people who can take generous views."

"Because it proves they are better. You yourself feel it does."

"Well, there might be a worse ambition. And it may make them so."

"It seems an arrogant one."

"Well, is there any ambition quite free from pride?"

"Now let me think about that," said Fanny, quoting her sister. "Perhaps some ambitions in themselves. None when they are realised."

"That seems to be deep."

"Yes, I thought it did. I tried to make it so."

"Mine has been to manage a house and bring up an orphan sister. There is no pride there."

"I think there seems to be," said Fanny.

"Well you said there was in all fulfilled ambition."

"And I think I seem to be right."

"You know it is my thirty-eighth birthday today?"

"Yes, or I should not have made you a gift."

"Do you see I am going grey at the temples? Oh, people do not notice such things."

"It is a kind they do notice. It reminds them that they are not going grey themselves. And if they are, they notice it more. They are waiting for it."

"Fanny, you do not mean half you say."

"Yes, often almost the whole."

"Grey hair is supposed to give people personality."

"It does, the appearance of it. And that is what you mean."

"Ah, there is the reason of the lateness," said Rhoda, going to the window. "Hamish seems hardly to have the strength to move. And Sir Edwin does not take his eyes off him. Ah, there is trouble there. How right we were not to judge!"

"And how generous you are! But it cannot be much comfort. It is true that things are wrong."

The sisters watched at the window, two upright, young women of ordinary height and build, with fair, straight faces, widely spaced eyes, and a likeness between them that seemed to emphasise the difference. Their clothes and hands and general suggestion told of a country life passed within the bounds of ease. Rhoda's dress was contrived with some cleverness, Fanny's better cut and simpler, and in no need of contrivance.

"Do you call Hamish Challoner 'Hamish' to his face?" she said.

"No, only in my mind. But it is in our minds that we live much of our life."

"I seem to live most of mine in this room. Not that that need make much difference. I wonder why the Challoner men come to see us."

"As the Challoner woman does not?" said Rhoda, smiling. "Why should she, if she does not wish? I have a feeling that Sir Edwin likes my friendship. I do not know why."

"I do. He ought to like it. It makes him feel he is wise, and so that you are."

"Well, I have my gleams of light. And if they can illumine the path of another, so much the better."

"I wonder how it feels to be soon to die. Would you be curious about the things you were not to know or see?"

"No, curiosity would not be my feeling. No, not just that."

"You would feel deeper things?"

"Yes, Deeper, wider, different," said Rhoda, looking before her.

"No wonder Sir Edwin thinks you are wise. He has no excuse for not doing so. If we pass over what is before our eyes, what is the good of its being there?"

"It may be just a little good, just a little."

"Well, we are laggards," said Sir Edwin, entering in front of his brother. "I fear that never might have been better than as late as this. We did not judge our time."

"We judged it," said Hamish, "but I did not make the pace. The never is far enough on the way for the lateness to be forgiven."

"Now you will tell us just how you are," said Rhoda.

"As I have done so, I will not again. Ill fortune does not add to us. And to be at one's end is nothing better. We can only be lessened by it."

"By being on the edge of the solution?" said Rhoda, looking down and just uttering the words, with a glance at Sir Edwin. "About to know the unknowable? No, no."

"I do not look to that. The dead past buries its dead. That is how it is about to serve me."

"The past and the future are alive. We add to them day by day. The present owes homage to them. And we in the present give it."

"Does your sister give her homage to anything?" said Hamish, smiling.

"Not to people's past," said Fanny. "There does not seem enough reason. They are too little pleased with it themselves. And not much to my own so far."

"We will pay homage to Fanny's youth," said Rhoda. "She is twelve years younger than I am. I remember the day when she was born."

"I am not sure that that is homage," said Hamish. "Do you pay it to anything, Edwin?"

"Sometimes to what is done or thought. Seldom to what comes of it."

"Ah, the lesson of our experience!" said Rhoda, turning towards him. "How I give it my homage! And some of what lies ahead! How we should bow before those who face it! There is the need for courage."

"It is good of you to see my place. And to see my brother's. I do not know which is the harder."

"I know. The one that demands the most. And you know, though you must not say it. When a thing is too much to face, we must accept it and be silent."

"Yes, it is too much for me. That is self-pity, and must be condemned. And I am uncertain how to feel to my brother. Pity of any kind has a poor name. And some of us would do ill without it."

"I feel no pity. What I feel is something else, something not even akin. I feel what I have said. As you confront things full and unafraid, you will remember that I feel it?"

"I am afraid. It is dark before me. I trust my own time

will not be long. That is the zenith of my hope. My brother and I have been too much to each other. We have given too little to our friends. I wonder we have them; we have but few. Life must be give and take."

"But it should be good to give. If we must take as well, it is a poor giving. We must render freely to make a gift. I hope I may give what I have? It is what I ask."

"So I shall have a friend. I shall need one and show my need. What I have will be less than nothing; you must indeed be willing to give. While I am waiting, I will remember. It will be a light in the coming blank. A faint one; I will say the truth; but it will be a light."

"I am grateful," said Rhoda, in a low tone. "And the fainter the light, the more grateful. To be allowed to do our little, when we cannot do much! It is indeed a cause for it."

"I can say no more. My brother is looking at us. I am his while he needs me. In a sense I am always his."

"We are talking of the future," said Hamish. "I find I like to think of it. When one will not share it, there is a lightness in its interest. I see it as a picture or a play."

"I see it as a threat," said Fanny. "There is more chance of ill than of good."

"Let us add your marriage to it. It is proper that a play should have one."

"Then I should have the loss," said Rhoda. "Not that that is a thing to count."

"Why is it not?" said Sir Edwin.

"You may marry yourself," said Hamish.

"Then the loss would be mine," said Fanny. "And I should count it, and expect other people to. I could not have anything I suffered, passed over."

"You would not mind pity?" said Sir Edwin.

"I should mind the case for it. I think people usually mind that the most."

"You are right not to be troubled by it. It can be of use."

"Why does marriage make loss?" said Rhoda. "It ought to widen a relationship, not weaken it."

"Widening things attenuates them," said Sir Edwin. "I think it has to be."

"It sounds as if people should not marry," said Hamish. "But permission is not sought. I have sons, and shall find it so. Or I should, if I were to see the time. It has yet to come."

"How are the sons doing?" said Rhoda.

"Thank you, not well. Simon is restless and dissatisfied, and Walter has left Oxford without a degree. I do not know how to help them in my days. And when I am elsewhere, it may only be permitted to help those who help themselves."

There was some mirth, and Rhoda spoke to Sir Edwin under its cover.

"We admire jesting about such things. We know it is brave and selfless; we should admire it. And yet we feel there is an emptiness beneath."

"My brother and I have no beliefs. No religious issue is involved. Death is to us the natural change and end."

"You have to be brave to face it, honest to feel it. Perhaps I could be neither. But I must stand by my own truth."

"It is not a question of courage, simply of what our reason accepts or denies."

"People talk as if we could select our beliefs," said Fanny. "They seem to think they are a matter of personal taste. And it is true there have been fashions in them, and that being out of fashion has been visited."

"Any honest belief is helpless," said Hamish.

"Oh, there is so much more in it than that," said Rhoda.

"I thought it put the matter in a word," said Sir Edwin.

"Yes, that is what it did. But is a word the right vehicle for anything with such a range, nothing less than the whole of human destiny?"

"Words are all we have. It is no good to find fault with them."

"And yet I do so. They are used as if they had some power. And how little they have!"

"I would not quite say that of yours," said Sir Edwin, smiling.

"Here are two people who will have opinions on the matter, indeed on all matters," said Hamish, as his sons were heard. "And they will not grudge them to us."

"We are not guilty of intrusion," said Simon, "or of any hope that we might be welcome. My mother has sent us to enquire for my father and to help him home. She was afraid he would find the second walk too much."

"Are you prepared to bear me in your arms?" said Hamish.

"Certainly, if there is need."

"I shall be glad of your support. I have come here for the last time, unaided. That is, for the last time. You must let me make the most of it."

"We will do the same," said Walter. "It is good to come out to tea without being asked."

"You may not have done that," said his father.

"But you perceive we have. Miss Graham is pouring it out. I am no longer affecting not to see."

"Is your mother troubled about me?"

"Not now you are in our charge."

"It is good to be a strong, young man," said Rhoda. "One of the best things."

"Not as good as that," said Walter. "We always have too little to our credit. A woman is not expected to have so much. It is enough that she exists."

"Oh, a good deal more is required of her than that. You would not like to be one?"

"Yes, I think I should. I should feel less guilt. And people say I should make a good-looking woman. Simon would make such an awkward one."

"My wife would have liked Walter to be a girl," said Hamish. "And I should have welcomed a daughter."

"No wonder I am guilty. That throws its own light."

"I should have liked a sister as well as a brother," said Simon.

"Simon, I hoped I was enough for you. The light grows fierce."

"I think you would make a good man, Rhoda," said Simon.

"I often have to be one. And I seem to manage fairly well."

"Simon, have you any reason to use Miss Graham's Christian name?" said Hamish.

"I have assumed I have tacit permission."

"Most things should be tacit," said Walter. "I often wish everything was."

"Ah, Walter's Oxford history makes a sad tale," said Hamish.

"Father, pray let it be tacit."

"You may depend too much upon that refuge."

"But let me do so enough."

"Come, I have said nothing yet."

"You said it in a word," said Simon.

"Well, if I went further, I might say too much."

"I don't think the term, tacit, seems much good," said Walter.

"You always seem so happy about things," said Fanny to Simon.

"It is useless to be crushed by them. It can do nothing. There is so much in front of us; my father's death, my mother's widowhood, my uncle's bereavement, my own dull and subservient life. There is no point in dwelling on it all, as if it were not enough."

"Your father is being brave. I daresay you wish he would be less so."

"I suppose he is; yes, of course he is. But I think cowardice is best," said Simon, laughing. "When my time comes, I shall be a coward. It will be better for me and everyone."

"I should be a coward anyhow. So much of one, that I doubt the usefulness."

"My father does what he owes to himself. I believe a lot

34

of virtue comes from that. His conception of himself is too high."

"Living up to it must be a strain. I should not think it is good for him."

"I am sure it is not. It is helping to shorten his life," said Simon, with his open acceptance of truth. "He should spare himself."

"My sister's conception of herself is also high. All her conceptions are. She would never see that cowardice was best."

"Perhaps our conception of ourselves is not as low as it might be," said Simon, laughing.

"What is not so?" said Hamish.

"Some people's conception of themselves, Father."

"I wonder how many of us would really say what that was," said Sir Edwin.

"I do not wonder," said Simon. "None of us."

"Oh, that is surely too sweeping," said Rhoda. "It might not be such an alarming thing."

"It would be," said Fanny. "We mean an honest conception, not a constructed one."

"Do we?" said Walter. "I was just constructing mine."

"I was checking my instinct to do so," said Hamish.

"His must be settled," said Simon to Fanny. "He has no time to modify it. And he would think it beneath him."

"And it is different for people without beliefs. We do not have to be fit to die."

"He has to be fit to be lamented and remembered. I sound callous, but that would be his thought. But his conception of himself is as honest as it can be. We can none of us look into the depths."

"Or what would be the good of having always kept our eyes from them?"

"It might be a wholesome experience," said Rhoda.

"Wholesome! What a strange word!" said her sister.

"You are giving a wrong impression of yourself. Or I trust you are."

"Well, I hope I seem to be."

"Do you believe in immortality, Rhoda?" said Simon.

"I can answer that in one word. Yes."

"I can do the same," said Fanny. "No."

"It should not be in us to feel we are born to die," said Rhoda. "We should be above such a feeling. Ah, it would be a poor conception, a poor thing."

"I agree that it is poor," said Simon.

"Should we like to live for ever?" said Hamish.

"Yes, if we did so," said his brother. "Our being would be adapted to it."

"It does seem that it might be done," said Walter.

"I seem to be obstinate," said Rhoda, "and that is said to be weakness. But I am not so sure."

"Neither am I," said Sir Edwin, smiling. "We may say it is weakness, when we find it too strong for us. Conviction is a powerful thing."

"We shall be thought argumentative sisters. That is, if people think of us."

"Oh, I hope they do that," said Fanny. "Why should we be ignored?"

Simon turned to her again.

"Do you like your life here with your sister?"

"Well, it is the life I lead. And I suppose we all like living."

"It does not afford you much scope."

"It affords me none. But what should I do, if I had it? The lack may be a protection."

"We cannot know what you could do, if you had the chance."

"Well, suppose we did know! It may be better not to find out."

"I should like to know it both about you and myself."

"Know what?" said Hamish.

"What we have in us, Father."

"Surely that emerges day by day."

"If it has a chance to do so."

"Oh, you do not wear fetters, my boy."

"I was wondering if both Fanny and I wore them in a way."

"We have no wings," said Hamish. "It is no good to feel we should spread them so far, if we had."

"I think it does us a little good," said Simon, laughing.

"We see where you get your poetic gift, Walter," said Rhoda.

"I hope he will make more use of it than I have," said Hamish.

"Father, surely your life has been a poem," said his son.

"I think we must be going. Your mother will be wondering about me."

"She said she would leave you in our hands," said Simon.

"I shall be in them in another sense, if we wait longer. And we have had what should be enough."

"As we have," said Rhoda. "We should ask no more. Indeed we do not ask it. We hope to come ourselves to you, when we may."

"It must be soon," said Simon, as he took his leave. "Or the visit will be too late, or of another kind."

"There is a pair of steadfast friendships," said Rhoda, looking after them. "How one hopes nothing will break them!"

"Something is to break one of them. There is no hope."

"I do not count death. That can break nothing. It may forge it stronger."

"It breaks everything. And broken things are not of use. They both know it."

"I am not sure about Sir Edwin. He seemed to be looking beyond the coming loss."

"Well, the time of suspense goes on, and his thoughts must go on with it, and go beyond. It was nothing more."

"Well, I will not read in too much. He was opening his mind to a friend. I was grateful for his seeing me as that."

"It is a thing he does seldom. I daresay to no one else. You were singled out."

There was a pause.

"Oh, what a dull, old-maidish life we must lead, to make so much of so little!" said Rhoda, lifting her hands. "Fanny, if you wanted to marry, you would not find me in the way? Thoughts of me I mean. Of course, I should not be, myself."

"We should both think of ourselves in such a case."

"And there would be someone besides ourselves."

"It seems to take two to do most things. To argue and to quarrel and to marry. Man is said to be a social creature. But it does not all seem so very social."

"We think more of Sir Edwin's loss than of Mrs. Challoner's. I do not know why."

"It will be the greater. And he will be left with nothing."

"Yes, she will have her sons," said Rhoda. "Somehow the family do not on the whole—seem as much affected by what is to come, as we might expect. I hardly know how to put it."

"It can be said in no other way. That is why I did not attempt it. I left it to you. I knew it was a thing that would break out."

"People can be greatly misjudged in such matters."

"And sometimes must be, as the verdict is always the same. They feel less than they ought to feel. If I died, it would be said of you, and if you died, of me. It will be said of one of us. It is quite disturbing."

"It will hardly be said of Sir Edwin."

"He is a person who will be expected to control his feeling. And so he may show less than passes muster. It is impossible to strike the mean, and the mean itself may be misjudged."

"Self-restraint is required and misinterpreted," said Rhoda. "But it may be that knowing so long beforehand will soften the edge of the grief. We can get used to anything."

"So time is to begin to heal the wound, before it is dealt. That will not be accepted."

38

"This is a slow, sure thrust, not a swift and sudden one. The healing must be different. And there will be young life about him, to make a stake in the future. Which do you like better, Simon or Walter?"

"Simon," said Fanny. "He has more to give."

"Is that a good reason?"

"It is a strong one, and it is mine."

"Have you more to give to him? That would be a better."

"Perhaps I have, as I like him the best."

"I should have thought Walter's poetry might make a bond between you."

"I did not say I admired it more than I did. And that broke the bond, or rather prevented it."

"I don't see why you should have said that."

"Well, it would have been putting his satisfaction before my own."

"Simon sometimes seems to me rather a heartless person."

"He is only honest," said Fanny.

"It can be heartless to be that, as you seem to have found."

"He shows what he is, and not many of us do."

"Surely you and I do. We have not so much to hide."

"About the usual amount. And we are wise to hide it."

"Then he might be wise to do the same."

"It appears that he might. But he does not do so. And people judge him by themselves, and think he must."

"You seem to know him very well."

"He is easy to know, as he wears no disguise."

"I cannot feel that I do, either."

"You have become used to doing it. You accept the picture you present."

"I don't think this talk means much."

"Too much. And it may mean more, if it continues."

"And there is something underlying it, that is not to my mind."

"If it underlies it, it would not be. That is why I like

Simon's talk. It has no hidden depths. And it tells you all it can."

"I think you mean depths that are not really hidden."

"I daresay I do. It is true that we are conscious of them."

"I think you are more guilty of them than I am."

"I daresay I am. I know I am very guilty."

"Fanny, you have many good qualities. Why do you cultivate the poor ones?"

"I do not. They stand in no need of it."

"You seem to push them to the fore."

"No, it is their natural place."

"I should like to see you make the most of yourself."

"As you have been doing. But I don't much enjoy the sight."

"Now is there something underlying that?"

"No, but it should have underlain it."

"You give a wrong impression of yourself."

"Do I? You think you have the right one."

"I sometimes feel you have not the true one of me."

"You mean the one that other people have."

"No, I mean what I say. Why should the two be different? And there is that underlying something again. Cannot you speak without it?"

"I do rather like speaking with it."

"You don't know how little it adds to you."

"So you think it does add something?"

"No, it takes more from you than it does from anyone."

"I don't think I did know that," said Fanny.

"It is unworthy to show off yourself at the expense of others. I do not mince my words. To say openly what is to be said! Ah, how much braver and better!"

"I think it is much worse. I can't tell you how bad it seems to me. And I never admire courage. It is always used against people. What other purpose has it?"

"I have said what I had to say. I shall not add another word."

"I hope not, unless you mince it," said Fanny.

# CHAPTER III

"SHALL I SOUND the gong to-night, as usual, ma'am?"

"Yes, I think so, Deakin. Life has to go on. It will not come to a standstill with our little lives. It will move on without us."

"It is as you say, ma'am. We are pawns in the game."

"Has Sir Edwin been by himself this afternoon?"

"Yes, ma'am, since the sad function. After a word to me he entered the library. And the door closed."

"We must try to do what we can for him. It will be better than thinking of ourselves."

"The one thing cannot be done, ma'am. Either for you or for him."

"I have my sons to help me."

"Yes, ma'am, the new generation cometh. It is coming now," said Deakin, with a faint smile, as voices sounded.

"Does Uncle know it is time for dinner?" said Walter.

"Not unless he has been told, sir. The thought will not suggest itself. But I am about to sound the gong."

"So the normal routine returns," said Simon. "And not before it is time. This paralysis of things has done no good."

"It is the usual observance, sir."

"The darkening of daylight and muting of sound! It is a savage survival. It strikes back into a primitive past."

"It may be the deeper rooted for that, sir. And life and death may be called primitive," said Deakin, as he went to the door.

"Deakin has followed the custom," said Julia. "It was what he could do. We will not criticise it."

"I will," said her son. "The oppression has made things worse. We are supposed to rise above a trouble, not to sink ourselves in it."

"We are hardly assumed to recover quite at once."

"A beginning must be made. And there it is! And my uncle's step is following. So normal cause and effect are working again."

"I hope I am not late?" said Sir Edwin.

"No, not at all," said Julia. "The gong has only just sounded."

"I thought perhaps it was a signal to me."

"To us all," said Simon. "It would have gone anyhow. Our life is as usual again."

"Will you carve to-night, Edwin? Or shall Simon do it for you?"

"I would depute it to Deakin first. But I will do it myself. As usual, as Simon would say."

"Oh, there is nothing in it," said his nephew. "It has become a habit to belittle what I do. It is time it ceased."

"Never mind about yourself to-day, my son," said Julia.

"To-day will pass. I shall have to be reckoned with. I am the only person now to follow my uncle, or to represent him, if he should fail. You must really know it."

"I do not pretend to forget what has happened, my boy."

"To forget its implications is to forget it in a sense."

"It has been remembered for five days," said Sir Edwin. "With the help of convention."

"We have the lights rather soon," said Walter, quickly.

"The dusk fell early, sir," said Deakin.

"Because we drew up the blinds?" said Simon, half laughing. "It tried to do our duty for us."

"Have you been tampering with—touching your father's papers, Simon?" said Sir Edwin. "They have been disturbed."

"I have been going through his accounts, Uncle, and following his method. You cannot do his work and your own. I must take his place."

"That is hardly a word to be said."

"It is a thing that must be done."

"You cannot expect to do it, Simon," said Julia.

"Not as a man, of course. In his work I hope I can. I must do my best."

"You should have waited for your uncle to suggest it."

"So it seems to us," said Sir Edwin. "But to him that time has passed. He has had his fill of waiting."

"I could not help my father's death. I would have done so, if I could."

"You are alone in saying so. You would not have been alone."

"The moths are falling into the lamps," said Walter.

"They come from the creeper," said Simon. "It grows apace."

"They come from the night, sir," said Deakin, in faint reproach. "There are none in the day."

"I don't know why we should suffer this oppression as well as our trouble."

"It comes from it," said Julia. "We are out of heart and hope. It is what has to be."

"It is not the way to help each other. I suppose we cannot really want to do that."

"I fear the words are true of you, my boy."

"I shall do what I can in my new place. Whether you like it or not, that is the word. It is senseless to make me feel guilty over it. You cannot be revenged on Fate by venting your feelings on me."

"It is a part of the truth," said his uncle.

"Well, you can feel that Father is watching you, Simon. That will help you to learn from him."

"Oh, I could not work under anyone's eye. And the level was not such a high one. I mean, not so high that another man cannot reach it. Why should it have been?"

"I cannot bear this speaking of your father in the past tense," said Julia, drawing in her shoulders.

"You are like my uncle. You resent my being his successor. It is a natural feeling, but he would not feel it a good one."

"You talk as if you were royal, Simon."

"You treat me as if I were. Neither of you is royal either. So you need not conspire against me, as if we were dynasts with a place in history."

"Simon, you are a very cultured man," said Walter.

"You were failing in respect to Father's memory," said Julia.

"His memory! What is that but speaking of him in the past tense? And we can hardly use any other. This is a feast for your ears, Deakin."

"It had not struck me in that light, sir."

"Well, you can listen or not, as you please."

"That again is hardly the expression, sir."

"My Walter has not much to say," said Julia. "Does he feel his brother has enough for two? I like to hear my sons talk, if they do it in a way that pleases me."

"We all like what is done in that way," said Simon.

"Simon, you have become so quick and sharp. I do not understand the change in you."

"There is no change. That is your trouble. You want me to be altered by my father's death. And I have not been, and shall not be. I am what I am."

"I cannot be that yet," said Walter. "I have not decided what it is. I should not dare to be like Simon. What do you feel you are, Uncle?"

"One elderly man out of many left alone. I hope you will never have to dare to be it. It needs the quality."

"You are not alone, Edwin," said Julia. "You have your brother's sons and me. And I don't feel he is far from us."

"I don't feel he is anywhere," said Simon. "I can't feel it. It is best to be honest about it."

"I wonder if it is," said Walter. "All these things you are, don't seem always to be best."

"If I felt that, I should not find life worth living," said Julia. "And I am sure your uncle would not."

"I feel it, and do not find it so," said Sir Edwin. "And I shall not."

"I feel it, and do find it so," said Simon. "And I am not ashamed of it. I think it is the braver thing."

"Simon! Surely you are ashamed," said Walter.

"I think we deserve something better," said Sir Edwin. "It is a meagre dole."

"What do you think, Deakin?" said Simon. "Were you listening?"

"I think I caught the words, sir."

"Well, what is your own feeling?"

There was a pause.

"Do we leave the mistress alone on her side, sir?" said Deakin, in a low, incidental tone, not raising his eyes.

"She does not want any pretence from us."

"No, sir?" said Deakin, in faint question.

"What if Father is near us, Simon, and knows what you think?" said Julia.

"He would understand it. It is what he thought himself."

"He must know better now."

"Well, in that case he realises we have not had his opportunities."

"Simon, I dislike this ironic note, if that is what it is."

"He likes it to be called that," said Walter.

Sir Edwin gave a faint laugh.

"Well, we shall start again tomorrow," said Julia. "And face a life full of difference."

"There must be many changes," said Simon. "There is the great one, and others must follow. One comes into my mind, Uncle. There is my father's way of keeping the rent accounts in one schedule, when the conditions vary. Do you think it would be well to alter it, while changes are being made?"

"It would be a surface difference, not a real one. And I am not thinking of changes."

"Do you object to my making this one?"

"Yes, but you may make it. I must see things go past myself; go onward, if that is the word. It is not in this case, or it is not mine. But make any pretence you will."

"Bitterness does no good, Uncle."

"None. But what you are doing will do none either."

"Simon," said Julia, "why have you started this way of saying 'my uncle' and 'my father' instead of 'Uncle' and 'Father'? It is quite a new thing."

"It is?" said Simon, with his laugh. "I suppose I have taken a step forward in my life. The ways of a boy are no longer mine."

"I admire your ease in answering such a question," said Walter. "I should have been most embarrassed. But I don't know whether to copy you."

"Be yourself, my boy," said Julia. "I am content to have you different. Simon will be my progressive son, and you my dependable one."

"But I am not sure that I am content."

"Your ways would always be those of a boy to me. And to me this last fancy of Simon's is really one of them."

"Then it seems I need not copy him," said Walter.

"The hall is as dim as the dining-room," said Simon, looking through the door. "It is that great bookcase in the middle. Do you like it there, Uncle? I have heard my father speak of moving it."

"You did not hear him order it to be moved. If you had, it would not be there. And you may come to have heard him speak of many things."

"If it was put at the back of the staircase, the hall would be twice the size."

"It would look so you mean, and that is overstated."

"We like it where it is, Simon," said Julia. "Or it would not have been there all these years. We want to keep all we can of our old life. That is the real one to us."

"I do not believe in this fear of change. If we can never change, we can never learn. I hope I shall go on learning all my life."

"We can make a change without learning," said Sir Edwin. "Indeed change may involve a certain forgetfulness."

"And it is to go on all Simon's life," said Walter.

"His changes may be good, or good to him. But the time for them is not yet. There is still a life in the way."

"I hoped it would not be, Uncle. I hoped you and I might make some improvements together. There are some that need to be made."

"Simon, your father and uncle would have made them, if they had seen them as such," said Julia. "I cannot think what has come to you. Your position is not altered. And if it was, it would be too soon to act upon it. You would hardly choose to-day."

"I was not thinking of the day. I was just saying what came into my mind."

"You can do that too much and too often. And some people would feel you might be thinking of the day."

"I usually suppress what comes into mine," said Walter. "And as for just saying it, I did not know that was ever done."

"I may be the better of the two," said Simon.

"I see no reason for thinking so," said his mother.

"Walter has suggested a reason."

"Have I?" said Walter. "What was it?"

"That my ideas were of a kind to be revealed."

"I am sure I did not suggest that, Simon."

"I see that difference between them," said Sir Edwin. "Simon is the more likely to expose himself. And that may imply that he has not much to hide."

"Uncle, pray do not hint things about me," said Walter. "I am such a defenceless person."

"I do not believe in this self-exposure," said Julia. "I think we have had enough."

"Would you like to be exposed, Deakin?" said Walter.

"Few of us would care to be completely, sir. We might be surprised ourselves."

"And that might not be the only consequence," said Julia. "Other people might be surprised, and show it!"

"I don't think they would be so surprised," said Simon, laughing. "Though of course they would not show that."

47

"Well, I should be glad for the self-revelation to cease. It goes further than you know."

"We always meet as much as is useful," said Sir Edwin.

"Edwin, that is how you spoke to Hamish. For a moment I felt I had you both with me again."

"I fear it was not for longer. And that it will not often be so."

"Simon," said Julia, "I wish you would not talk so often to Deakin. He will get into such odd ways."

"Oh, he has been with us so long. And he only answers when he is spoken to. He never enters into the talk."

"He can hardly do one without the other. And it is you I am criticising, not him."

"Well, cease your criticism. I am tired of it. I seem to hear nothing else. You often talk to Deakin yourself. He is your intimate friend."

"He is a good friend to us all. I am the last to deny it. But that does not alter what I said."

"It was Walter who spoke to him this last time."

"My dear boy, you cannot think that makes a difference."

"Deakin," said Simon, as the former returned, "do you like the position of that bookcase in the hall? Would you not rather see it behind the stairs?"

"I should not see it there, sir. It would not strike the eye. And I feel it has a claim to its place. It is like the appeal of a dumb animal."

"Why are animals called dumb?" said Walter. "No one thinks they can speak."

"They can anyhow move," said Simon, "and the book-case cannot. It looms before one like a cloud. We seem to be cultivating gloom."

"It is not a moment when we should be so cheerful," said his mother.

"You know what I meant. Why do you pretend you do not? You misjudge me on purpose. It is a second-rate thing to do."

"I must sometimes judge you, my son. You rather lay yourself open to it."

"Just because I want the house as cheerful as I can have it. As you imply, we have no other kind of cheer."

"It is not for you to take the lead. Your uncle will suggest any changes he wishes."

"But he will not wish for any, even those that cry out to be made. We shall go on and on in the same way."

"It is what we shall do," said his uncle. "If you can call it the same."

"There it is again. You give my words a wrong meaning. You should be ashamed of it."

"I was confusing the kind of sameness, it is true. I am not at my best."

"And Simon is not at his," said Julia. "I think he is upset by the day in his own way."

"It is not in anyone else's."

"And my Walter is silent. We are none of us ourselves."

"Simon seems somehow to have come into his full self."

"When a part is always better," said Walter. "And he should be upset by the day in other people's way."

"Well, you know the worst about me now," said his brother.

"And we do not about them. You see their way is best."

"Shall I take coffee into the drawing-room, ma'am?" said Deakin.

"Perhaps Sir Edwin would like his alone in the library."

"No, I must ask more of you. I cannot be alone. And I am fit for nothing else."

"I am glad you have asked something. I was wondering if you ever would. And I am afraid a good deal has been asked of you. We will all have coffee in the library, Deakin, as Sir Edwin likes that room. Simon, will you see that your uncle's chair is in its place?"

Simon did so, waited for his mother to take the opposite one, and when she did not do so, took it himself.

"Simon, would you sit there?"

"Why not? We do not want the place empty."

Julia glanced at her brother-in-law.

"It does not matter. Nothing matters or alters the truth. Nothing can press it further home to me. But I should have thought the place was yours."

"To me it is Hamish's. I would rather sit here. And I should have thought it would be his to Simon too."

"Well, I represent him now," said her son. "He cannot have it himself. And we do not want chairs empty, as if they were occupied by ghosts."

"I could almost feel that your father's spirit was there."

"Well, I suppose it might be, according to your belief."

"Julia, will you take the chair?" said Sir Edwin. "And may it be yours in future?"

"Well, I daresay my father would rather share it with her than with me," said Simon, as he relinquished it.

"Simon, I don't know what has come to you," said Julia.

"What has come to us all. My father's death. He has no place any longer. In losing his life he has lost what it held. Nothing can affect him. Nothing can be his. You must really know it."

"His wife's heart is his," said Julia.

"That is saying the same thing in a different way."

"I agree that it is different," said Walter.

"I might say that my heart is his," said Simon. "I had a sincere feeling for him."

"But do not say it, Simon," said his brother.

"I shall always think of my early years with him. But a show of sentiment has no meaning."

"I think it may have a great deal," said his mother. "I never believe much in things that are not shown. If we are left to imagine them, they may be imaginary."

"My uncle is not showing so much."

"Simon, you know better than to say that. I wonder you can utter the words."

"What is it? I did not hear," said Sir Edwin, turning his head.

"It was not worth your attention," said Julia.

"Those books are covered with dust," said Simon, who was walking about the room. "They cannot have been done for days."

"Your father dusted them himself. The bindings are old and delicate. He did not like the servants to touch them."

"I will do them," said Simon, taking out a handkerchief.

"No, no, Simon, you will be too rough."

"I am the last person to be so. The books will be mine one day. And the duty is surely a simple one."

"Have you asked your uncle's permission?"

"Why should I? He has not dusted them. You and Walter have not. It appears that the servants may not. Is it to be left to my father's spirit?"

"Simon, I am ashamed of you. Go out of the room."

Simon smiled and continued his task.

"He does it as his father did," said Sir Edwin, in an empty tone. "There will be no harm."

"There!" said Simon, folding the handkerchief. "There is a true word at last."

"I want something to dust," said Walter, looking round.

His uncle gave a little laugh.

"One of us will do them every day," said Simon.

"The matter will be as your uncle wishes," said Julia.

"Matters can go on in front of me. I will not check them. There is no time or need."

"You are patient with Simon, Edwin."

"We see how patient he has had to be, and still has, and will have to be."

"We have to look beyond a single life," said his nephew.

"At yours you mean. It may be left to you."

"I hope this is not the real Simon," said Julia.

"I am showing the depths within me. You are doing the same. And I may be as surprised as you are."

"That is unfair and untrue," said Sir Edwin.

"Are there depths in you, Deakin?" said Walter.

"Well, sir, I must own there are. And they have stood revealed at times."

"I should be nervous of seeing it."

"It is hardly on that scale, sir. Merely a forgivable outbreak."

"I have not met that kind. And I don't think I could forgive it. I suppose it is like lovable weaknesses. I find them so unlovable."

"Have you none of your own?" said Simon.

"I think the whole of me is weakness. But I am almost sure it is lovable."

"Simon, you are only pretending to read," said Julia.

"Yes," said her son, laughing. "I am upset by the recent scene. Future generations will not realise what they owe to me. Debts to the past are forgotten."

"And they are usually to the past," said Walter. "And then they prevent our incurring them in the present."

"I don't know what to think of my sons," said Julia. "I have no husband to help me with them now."

"Well, we know that," said Simon. "You have not made a discovery."

"I hope you will remember it, and make things easy for me."

"I thought a woman's path was always hard," said Walter.

"A widow's is," said his mother.

"So we belong to the widow and the fatherless. I feel that is dignified of us."

"I think it is pitiful," said Simon. "And we are forgetting my uncle."

"I am not," said Julia. "I would as soon forget the two of you."

"I have no claim on remembrance," said Sir Edwin.

"You must try to be one of us, Edwin. Or you will be alone in your own house."

"That is what I must be. None of you is to blame."

"Simon has not been himself today. You must not let him estrange you from us."

52

"We have had new glimpses of him. I think not yet the whole."

"It is not my fault that I shall have more scope now," said his nephew.

"Simon! I hope this is the whole," said Walter.

"How else could I put it?"

"Surely differently," said Julia.

"He said what he meant," said Sir Edwin. "Other words would have had other meaning."

"I would have chosen to hear them. Where are you going, Edwin?"

"Out for a while. And perhaps to the Grahams. I need a word with a friend."

"There, Simon!" said Julia, as the door closed. "What a thing to hear, when he is with his own family! I hope you will learn the lesson. And on this day of all others!"

"Should I be apt to learn on that day? Is it a mental stimulus? You seem to think it should encourage every good quality. You will end by being thankful to it."

"I shall have little reason. And you might have been such a help to me."

"I have been more than you know. The day will come when you realise it."

"So Simon has been misunderstood," said Walter. "And it will be found out in his lifetime. I did not know that ever happened. And he has told us himself; and I am sure that never does."

"Well, we must understand him in future," said Julia, putting an arm about her son. "I think his mother has done so, but he makes it hard for other people. And now let us talk about your father, and resolve to follow where he led. That will help us with our first steps in the new life."

"Has not Simon taken his?" said Walter. "I was trusting they were behind."

"Now when your uncle returns, Simon," said Julia, an hour or two later, "remember he lives in a past you do not understand. To him the old ways are best."

"And if they are not, must I wait for his death to see it? It would mean I did wait for it, and that is a poor enough thing."

"I am not talking about his death, but about his life. He has a future, as you have; and there is no reason to look beyond it. It is a thing that is never done."

"Never openly you mean. That is the difference between me and other people. I am not an overreaching person. I don't know why you think so."

"I am glad you are not, Simon," said Walter. "It is a great relief."

"It is no credit to you to be the elder son. You must not stand too much on it. Somehow I did not think our talk today would be like this."

"I know what you thought it would be. I am glad it is not."

"It would have been better to look back on."

"It would have meant we could never do so."

"Well, bear one thing in mind. Your uncle has the first claim on us. And you must not expect him to be your mother."

"We don't even think he may be a father to us. And perhaps he should try to be that."

"Well, in that case you should be sons to him."

"Oh, I think he has been upset enough," said Simon, laughing.

"You can try to put yourself in his place."

"That is the last thing he wants. He does not even like my being in my own."

"You know what I meant. You must look at things through his eyes."

"In that case I must try not to see myself," said Simon.

"Your doing so might be a help to both of you."

"I don't dare to imagine it all," said Walter. "Simon will suggest things, and be honest, and will not be Father. I don't see how Uncle will bear it."

"Bear what?" said another voice, as Sir Edwin returned.

"Working with my son," said Julia.

"It is not a change I have chosen. He knows that, and will ease it for me. And I am old to make it. And that is a thing he knows."

"You must not make a study of Simon, Uncle," said Walter. "You cannot work with anyone you understand."

"I should have thought that would make it easier," said Julia.

"I am a simple person to follow," said her elder son.

"But we will not say anything about that, Simon," said Walter.

"I think you look better for your walk, Edwin," said Julia.

"Yes, the night was kind, and the friends also. We are helped by kindness."

"Dear Edwin, you are very brave. I must tell you once that I think so."

"A woman is able to say those things," said Simon.

"A woman can forget herself," said his mother.

"Men would feel it too simple to say a thing of that kind."

"Well, that is not forgetting themselves," said Walter.

"There are things women see more easily," said Sir Edwin. "Or more often."

"You think so, Edwin?" said Julia. "I have thought you preferred men."

"I do not put one above the other. It is a thing people are too apt to do."

"Did you find my father ready to forget himself, Uncle?" said Simon.

"Simon, only you could put such a question at such a time," said Julia.

"I think I need not answer it," said Sir Edwin.

"Do Rhoda and Fanny feel my father's death?"

"Yes, but not first for themselves," said his uncle, turning away.

"I fear your uncle is beyond help," said Julia, in a low tone. "And of course I am too in a different way."

55

"I am glad it is not the same," said Simon. "He might take a lesson from you, if it were worth while at his age."

"When you come to the age, you will think less of it."

"I shall think more," said Walter. "I shall be so near to the grave."

"You may die at any age," said his brother.

"No, I shall live to the full span. And every year will take from it."

"Mater, it is strange that we think of my uncle's loss more than of yours," said Simon.

"Well, I have my sons. And I gave your father up to his brother in a way. It was a thing I could do for both of them. It was a good thing I could do myself. I have not done enough good things in my life."

"No wonder my uncle balks at trouble, when he is used to such dealings. I suppose you would give both of us up to him, if he needed us. Not that there is any likelihood of it."

"I will not make the claim," said Sir Edwin, with a faint smile. "I must serve my own need. It is true that I have not hidden it."

"And what of your need, Mater? Of course you have your sons, but he does not rank that compensation high."

"How high do I rank it?" said Julia, smiling and giving him her hand.

Simon leant back with it in his, and glanced about him.

"Four seems a comfortable number," he said.

"Simon, think what you are saying!" said Julia.

"I am thinking. My father and uncle sat apart. There were the three of us together. And now my uncle has joined us."

"You should remember the reason of the change."

"So you feel it is possible to forget it?"

"You might almost make us think it was. You should be careful what you say."

"I dislike people who have to do that. I have nothing to hide. It is better to talk honestly."

"I think it is much worse," said Walter. "It means all

sorts of risks. Honest people can even say: 'If you don't mind my saying so,' after they have said it. And they cannot know before. Dishonest talk is far better. I should like to hear myself described insincerely."

"What do you think, Edwin?" said Julia.

"I am afraid I did not hear."

"You are tiring your uncle," said Julia, to her sons.

"No, I was lost in my own thoughts. It sounds egotistic, and is what it sounds."

"Would you like to be alone?" said Julia, gently.

"I will remain in the flesh and be absent in spirit, if you will bear with it."

"We like to have you with us in any sense. I am often sunk in my thoughts too."

"Mater, you set an example," said Simon. "You have your own change to face. You are making a brave beginning."

"So honest conversation can be as good as this," said Walter. "I must think of something honest to say."

"Was my uncle absent in the spirit, when he was with Rhoda and Fanny?" said Simon, lowering his tone. "And did he tell them he did not hear what they said? They must have wondered why he called on them."

# CHAPTER IV

"I HAVE SOMETHING to say to you," said Sir Edwin, remaining at the table after a meal. "I am going to be married tomorrow to Rhoda Graham. I have not told you before. I will not say more than the one word now. I do not accept the idea of discussion or question. We shall be alone at the marriage, go from it on a short journey, and return in about two weeks. I have ordered the room next to mine to be prepared."

There was a pause.

"Hamish's room?" said Julia, saying what came to her lips.

"The room that was his. It is a better room than mine."

There was another pause.

"Who will be the mistress of the house?" said Simon, in a sudden tone.

"My wife," said his uncle.

"After my mother has been so for twenty-seven years?"

"After that. And after it, she is able to help another in the place. I will ask it of her."

"I am glad you are to have more in your life, Edwin," said Julia, in a fainter tone. "We are all glad."

"You have been a friend to me, Julia. I will not ask you to be one now. It would be to throw doubt upon it. You will see that my life is my own."

"Our lives are never our own," said Simon. "They are bound up with other lives. They belong in part to other people."

"They cannot move along a line with no crossroads. And one is here."

"Rhoda's life would be joined to one that has had its

58

past, and may have no future. In other words she would share it in its last stage."

"She will, you might say. And the first words would have served you."

"Simon, that will do," said Julia, in a low tone.

Sir Edwin rose from his seat.

"I will say the word I owe to you. You have a right to hear my reasons for a change in my life, that must bear on yours. I cannot live by myself amongst those who live in fellowship. I must have a semblance of it. I need it in order to face the time before me. I do not choose to say more."

There was a pause.

"Do you wish us to remain in the house, Uncle?" said Simon.

"I am willing that you should."

"I am glad my mother has not to seek another home. I infer that you do not think of having a family?"

"I have said that I do not accept the idea of question."

"It must all be said, when you have left us. Would it not be better to say it to your face?"

"I do not know why that should improve it," said Sir Edwin, going to the door. "Nor need I hear it, to know what it will be."

"Well, we will say it behind his back," said Walter. "So that he cannot really know."

"We have not given him companionship," said Julia, in a slow tone. "But it has been hard to give it. He has shrunk into himself. He has needed to be first with someone. It is what he has been."

"You did what could be done," said Simon. "More was not due from you or due to him."

"He would not always have had it, if it had not been due in a way."

"Well, what a shock for all of us! But if there is to be no family, the future remains the same. There will simply be Rhoda's provision after my uncle's death."

"Simon, must you still harp on that? You must see it is his life, that is in question now."

"I only meant there would be a limit to the change."

"None to the changes. The house will be hers, and I shall be here to help her in it. I shall be a mere member of the household, after being its mistress for so long. But I have had no claim to the place."

"You have earned it by filling it for all these years. There is such a thing as the right of tenure."

"We see that there is not."

"It cannot be true," said Walter. "Now I know what it is to feel I am living in a dream. And I hardly want to wake. I feel a sort of excitement."

"It is the shock," said his mother. "The feeling will not last."

"We might have foreseen it," said Simon. "He has been going so often to the Grahams. And they have not come here. We might have deduced something from it. We were not to see them together. Of course I know it is wisdom after the event."

"But when it is so much wisdom," said Walter, "it cannot matter when it comes."

"We must not have a sense of grievance," said Julia. "What we have had was not ours by right. Your uncle might have married in his youth."

"Then my father would not have lived in his house," said Simon. "We should have had a home of our own. We see now that we have never had one. And my father might have worked for himself instead of merging his life in his brother's. We cannot ignore the history of two lives."

"I shall have no right to exist," said Walter. "What a good thing I have learned to be a burden!"

"What will Fanny do in that house by herself?" said Simon. "I suppose the best she can, as we shall in this one, not by ourselves."

"What do you say to it all, Deakin?" said Walter.

"It is hardly my place to comment, sir."

"I suppose you think the more?"

"That is said, sir, but I see no reason. Sometimes people who say less, think less also."

"But that is not true of you," said Julia.

"I must try to make it so, ma'am. Mr. Hamish's place is filled," said Deakin, turning to the door.

"Now I see no reason for keeping back the tears," said Walter. "Cry, Mater; it will do you good."

"I suppose it is to be a formal marriage," said Simon. "My uncle implied there would be no issue. And there are to be two rooms. I think we can be sure of our ground there."

"We cannot be sure of anything," said his mother. "An hour ago we should have been sure of different things."

"When my uncle dies, it will be Rhoda who meets the change. She has her place only for his life. The house will be mine, and you its mistress until I marry. Then you will share it with my family and me. We shall be more dependent on your income, with the demand for Rhoda's widowhood."

"Simon can only conceive of Rhoda as a widow," said Walter. "She is not to begin as one."

"Well, where I am, my sons will be," said Julia. "I must be grateful for that."

"I do not envy Rhoda her homecoming," said Simon.

"And her meeting with us after these secret dealings."

"She will have support," said his mother. "And it is not all she will have."

"I should have thought she would give up more. Her own life and her home and her sister. Though of course they will be waiting for her, when she returns."

"At your uncle's death," said Julia. "Is it never to be out of your thought? It is their life together that concerns them, not hers or ours when it is past."

"She has an income of her own. I don't know how she will use it. She may help Fanny with her house. We cannot say how things will be."

"They are not your concern, and must not appear to be."

"We shall live our days over a morass of apprehension and suspense. I wonder how we shall manage in them."

"We shall only have to live them," said his mother.

"I wonder that Fanny has not come to see us and discuss it."

"Surely you do not. It would not be permitted. And we see the reasons."

"My uncle has gone too far in subordinating everything to himself. I shall think so to the end."

"He has had the opportunity," said Walter. "I expect people always use it. Think how you are looking forward to using yours."

"When I am dead," said Sir Edwin, as he returned. "And in the meantime I am to live. He is not in a satisfying place."

"I shall be, Uncle, if I may continue to be of use to you."

"You can, as you know. There will be further need for your help."

"I will do my best, Uncle."

"Has a great change come over Simon?" murmured Walter.

"Do you want any packing done for you, Edwin?" said Julia.

"Thank you. Deakin has done what I needed."

"So Deakin has been in your confidence?" said Simon.

"Simon's true nature is not dead," said his brother.

"He has known I am going away," said Sir Edwin.

"But not with whom you were going?" said Simon.

"I have not told him more than I said."

"And he has not told us anything. That shows he has known the whole."

"There is nothing so strange about a marriage. It is an ordinary thing."

"That is hardly true of this one. But you have every right to enter into it, as you do not need to be told."

"It is true that the words are wasted. And there are others I need not have heard. When I return, I will hear no more of them. That means you will say no more."

"What will Fanny do in that house by herself?" said Simon, not looking at his uncle.

"What other people do in similar case. And she will have a foothold in her sister's home."

"I can't help the whole thing's being strange to me, Uncle."

"Then you will be the person apart, as she will not."

"We have not congratulated you, Edwin," said Julia. "We were taken by surprise. You know we do so from our hearts."

"Thank you. You have always served me. I owe much to you."

"Your life with my father for twenty-seven years," said Simon. "You will never feel that anyone fills that place."

"My wife is to do something different, fill a place of her own."

"No doubt you needed someone in your life, who belonged wholly to you. You had always had it."

"You are right as far as you go. It is further than you have gone."

"I hope I have not failed in sympathy, Uncle?"

"It has not been in my mind to ask it. Or in yours to give it."

"I begin to have a feeling of guilt."

"It is not your fault that I have not done so. But I have seen no reason."

"I have not meant to put my life before yours."

"Our own lives are first to us. You see that mine is to me. And you should understand it. It is something we learn from ourselves."

"Simon, you will weary your uncle," said Julia.

"I am tired, it is true. I will go and rest. I am travelling tomorrow."

"Deakin," said Simon, "you did not tell us that Sir

63

Edwin was going to be married. You kept the knowledge to yourself."

"I had none at first, sir, except by inference. And Sir Edwin was the one to impart it."

"I expect you dreaded the moment for us."

"Well, for the mistress, sir," said Deakin, lowering his voice and glancing at Julia. "It is not to be a slight change."

"I must not be called the mistress much longer," said Julia.

"No, ma'am, I have seen the matter in its bearings."

"And this is the worst to you?" said Walter.

"I could not apply the term to another, sir."

"You will have to, Deakin," said Julia. "It will be better for us all."

"It will be lip service, ma'am."

"Well, that is a kind that is recognised," said Walter.

"Have you talked of the matter to Sir Edwin?" said Simon.

"Not to say that, sir. I merely had the information."

"But no doubt you showed surprise?"

"I hope not unduly, sir. I try to fulfil my calling, as I see it."

"I have a great respect for it," said Walter.

"Yes, sir, it is what is said."

"It is a great deal to say," said Julia. "And it is what we feel for the most important things."

"But not the need to say it, ma'am. There being no need."

"What will Rhoda feel about her position here?" said Simon. "It must seem such a temporary thing."

"She will live in the present, as we shall," said Julia. "Well, the past is safe, and much of my life is there."

"I wish I could know what my father would say to it. Do not you, Deakin?"

"It is a wish I can hardly feel, sir."

"It may be that he knows," said Julia.

"Then I wish I could know what he does say, and to whom he says it," said her son.

"Sir Edwin is doing nothing wrong, Deakin," said Julia.

"Well, ma'am, the words cover a wide ground."

"You think he essentially is?" said Simon.

"Well, sir, if he had left things as they were, he would have remained where he was. He seems to have left his place. Though it is not for me to feel it."

"It is a pleasant thing to hear. I am tired of being the one person to speak the truth."

"I think we all stand together, sir. It is what is left."

"Miss Graham will be Lady Challoner," said Walter. "Had you thought of that?"

"Yes, it had struck me, sir. And I once hoped to use the words. But the years passed, and the mistress had the place. Now the time is late."

"It sounds like Shakespeare," said Walter.

"Well, sir, I understand he portrayed life. And that is what it is."

"Everything comes into it," said Julia.

"Yes, ma'am. It is a comprehensive term."

# CHAPTER V

"I HAVE NEVER FELT less at ease," said Julia. "How am I to yield a position that has never been mine? I cannot think of an example."

"And not to be at ease is so humbling," said Walter. "If only the cup would pass from us!"

"Walter, such words are not for our own lives."

"But it is in those that things happen to us. There is nothing anywhere else."

"It is no good to be clever at this moment," said Simon.

"Oh, I thought it was rather brave."

"What would my father say to the scene? We must ask ourselves that question."

"He might in a way be glad of it," said Julia. "He would not wish his brother to be alone."

"It is a noble answer," said Walter.

"I suppose he would expect him to be," said Simon. "It is in a sense a debt to be paid."

"He was not a person to exact payment," said Julia.

"But he might accept it," said Walter. "And no one could expect anyone to get over his death."

"There may be no question of that. People may fill a place, because they cannot bear to have it empty."

"I would not put up with it. Mine is to be filled with my memory."

"That is the trouble," said Simon, almost sighing. "A place has to be filled with something. And memories are at once not enough and too much."

"Simon, you sometimes show us your real self," said Julia.

Deakin came swiftly and silently through the hall.

"The sound of wheels!" said Walter. "How they are the heralds of fate!"

"Now here is my welcome," said Rhoda's voice. "To the family to which I belong, of which I am to be a part. I feel I shall become one. I shall find my place."

"It is surely prepared for you," said Simon.

"No, I am to make it. As yet it is not mine. It is a thing I must do for myself."

"We have wished you were here oftener," said Julia. "Now the wish is to be fulfilled."

"It is a kind word. It falls on a grateful ear. Kindness at some moments does and means so much."

"Would you like to come at once and see your room?"

"If it is mine, if it is no one else's. I will take it from no one. It is for me to prove my claim."

"It was my husband's. He liked to be near his brother."

"Then he would wish me to be so. He would yield the place. He would see me as the substitute that I am, the thing I am proud to be."

"We are forgetting your existence, Uncle," said Simon.

"It is a moment when you may do so."

"You know us better than that, Edwin," said Julia.

"Well, it can be said of you and me."

"Would you wish to have tea before you go upstairs, my lady?" said Deakin.

"If that is when Mrs. Challoner has it."

"It is to be as you say," said Julia.

"No, as you do, as it has always been. I am a member of your household, one of the many who look to you."

"That is what Rhoda wishes," said Sir Edwin. "She will not alter the order of things. It is to be in your hands, as it has been."

"Yes, that is the basis of the future," said his wife. "The roots have gone down. They are too deep to be disturbed."

"You are sure it is your wish?" said Julia. "Of course you can change at any time. You can easily say the word."

"I shall not say it. My word is said."

"Will you pour out the tea? Or shall I be your deputy today?"

67

"You will do it for me, and all of us. Today and other days. As it was, so it is to be."

"Where would you like to sit?"

"At the side by Edwin, where his brother sat. If I may have the place, if it prove to be mine."

"Well, everything is settled," said Sir Edwin. "And nothing more need be said. Simon, I can give you some time later, if you need my help."

"Everything can wait until tomorrow, Uncle."

"There is no reason for it. We can return to our usual ways."

"It is good to have them," said Rhoda. "They are what we need. I shall be grateful to share them, to make them my own."

"And you will have something to give to us," said Simon. "And we shall be the better in our turn."

"Not as much as I shall be. It is I who take and do not give."

"You will be glad to see your sister," said Julia.

"My Fanny, my little one! It is what I shall be. It is the thing I ask of you, a welcome for her. Then the house will be my home."

"I think I know how you like your tea," said Julia.

"It is for you to remember, to care for those dependent on you. You see me as one of them."

"I am spellbound by the scene," murmured Walter. "I did not know such things could be."

"What did you say?" said Sir Edwin.

"I said it was an unusual scene, Uncle."

"It is not a scene," said Rhoda. "It is something else. It is the filling of a blank, or rather a disguise of it."

"It depends on what sense we give the words," said Sir Edwin.

"To disguise a lack helps someone to suffer it. When to face it might be too much."

"You are here in a spirit of courage," said Simon, in a lower tone.

"I know what is asked of me. I am here to give it. I will not wish it was more. The risk would not be only mine."

"I am going round the garden," said Sir Edwin, with a hint in his voice that the scene was at an end. "If Rhoda will come with me, I shall not go alone."

"Well, this is our gain," said Julia, looking after them. "We shall not see him pacing those paths by himself. I have been afraid to look out of the window."

"I am afraid to now," said Walter. "I do not dare to face the sight. Are they walking close together?"

"Side by side, as your uncle is used to walking," said his mother.

"There is a strangeness about everything. It is untrue in a deep sense."

"Rhoda is sincere," said Simon. "And she is wise not to undertake the house. It will be easier for her to withdraw, when the time comes."

"Simon, you are beyond all hope," said Julia. "And I agree that the scene was strange. There was something unreal in the surprise of it. I suppose I am right in taking her at her word?"

"There is nothing to question about her. She is doing her best for my uncle and all of us. She can hardly do more."

"But is it what is good for herself? It will leave her at a loose end. She will have time on her hands. Your uncle has not much to spare."

"She has her own resources. She has had to make them. The truth is that we are fortunate. Things might have been so different. With anyone else they would have been."

"Do not like her too well," said Walter. "She belongs to Uncle, not to you."

"Oh, their relation is not romantic. I know what it is. Indeed she herself has told us. She admires and pities my uncle. How could anyone not do so? It is worth her while to succour him, and have him in his last years. Many women might have felt it. But she was the woman he knew."

"And what does he feel?" said Julia. "You have so much wisdom, that you must share it."

"He was lonely and aloof from us. He wanted someone for himself. She was a substitute for my father, the likely person, the one at hand. We have few people in our life."

"Why did he not turn to me," said Walter, "and ask me to be a son to him?"

"Why you and not me?" said Simon.

"Well, Simon, what are your filial qualities?"

"I am more in the position of a son, as I am to succeed him."

"And you think that feeling fits you for the place?"

"Now, Simon," said Julia, "I forbid you to refer again to your uncle's death, to anything before or after it, to the death itself. And I expect to be obeyed."

"I am to forget the future and live in the present? Well, perhaps it offers more than it did."

"Rhoda is meeting the crisis as well as she can. It is pleasant not to have to criticise her."

"So that is what you had in your mind," said Simon.

"I was looking forward to it," said Walter. "There is a general sense of blank."

"There is in a sense," said his brother. "There is no feeling of anything to come. And something must be coming. We are to have a different life, and can only await it."

"It will go on, as lives do," said Julia. "Mine will be the one apart. I shall grow into an old woman, while you move into your prime. And I shall do it without my husband."

"You exaggerate the tragedy of widowhood," said Simon. "It is a common enough thing."

"Yes, my dear, and so is all sickness and suffering. The commonness of a thing leaves it as it is."

"It must alter the attitude towards it. We cannot respond too much. We should be worn out."

"Your mother's life should count to you, I suppose. You can respond to that."

"Mater, your widowhood is not a new thing. Why should it take on this sudden growth?"

"It is a thing that is fresh with every day, my boy."

"Well, so is the daylight and the dark."

"Yes, and widowhood belongs to the last. And this marriage may take your uncle's friendship from me. For all this resolve to alter nothing, it may do that."

"They are coming to the house," said Walter. "Still walking side by side. And his hand might have been resting on my head. It is astonishing that he never thought of it."

"Never thought of what?" said Sir Edwin.

There was silence, and Simon gave a laugh.

"It cannot be repeated? Let it rest, if it does not bear it."

"Uncle, my mother is here. Should I utter a word that was not fit for her ears?"

"It was unfit for mine? Or rather, it was not meant for them."

"Why should it have been, Edwin?" said Julia. "You were not in the room. It was a piece of boyishness."

"You grant us perennial youth, Mater," said Simon. "We are always children to our mothers."

"It is good to be with a family," said Rhoda. "To hear men talk as women never do, and women as men never do. It is a good thing."

"Is there so much difference?" said Julia.

"The difference there has to be, that we want there to be, that there is."

"And what is that?" said Simon.

"You do not need me to say. You are of those who know."

"Are we all among them?" said Walter.

"There is so much wisdom here. In the words, in the minds of those about me. I have come to its home."

"How will you spend your spare time here?" said Simon.

"Simon, there is one of your odd questions," said Julia. "How does any of us do so? It needs no answer."

"It shall have one," said Rhoda. "I shall be with you, listen to you, learn from you. And when Edwin comes, I shall be with you and him. How shall I spend my time? I shall not have enough."

"I will release him as often as I can," said Simon.

"It is I who will order things," said his uncle. "It is still my place."

"There is not enough work for both of us all the time."

"Then it is for you to be set free."

"That is the wrong way round, Uncle."

"It seems to me the right one. It is only my own opinion."

"Your sister will be with us soon, Rhoda," said Julia. "We knew you would wish it; we wished it ourselves; and she was able to come."

"Then I wish for nothing; I ask for nothing; I am grateful for each thing."

"If she will come in and out as one of us," said Sir Edwin, "she will serve us all."

"People with nothing to wish for are said to be dissatisfied. I am not of them."

"We shall be equal men and women at the table," said Simon. "It will be a change for my mother. She has been a woman by herself."

"Ah, change has come to you. It has come to me. We welcome or suffer it. It still comes."

"It would hardly do not to have it. Do you think it is a good thing, Uncle?"

"It is not in itself to me. I am an old man. I welcome what is of help."

"Here is Fanny already coming to us," said Julia.

"My little one, my sister. We are closer for being apart. We have more to give to each other; we have more to share. You have not been alone. You have been with me, carried in my heart."

"I would rather be with you in this room," said Fanny. "I like a more usual resting-place."

"I hope that means you will often be here," said Sir Edwin.

"Your voice is tired, Uncle," said Simon.

"Ah, it is. It must be," said Rhoda. "We have made our journey to you. We have had our welcome, had our hour. He has lived it for himself and me. Yes, he is tired."

"It is true," said Sir Edwin. "And I carry a double weight of years."

"I think you have borne up surprisingly, Uncle," said Simon.

"It continues to surprise you? And the feeling has yet to grow. It must become more with time."

"It was an innocent speech, Uncle."

"Yes, it was without art."

"You cannot expect me to forget the gulf between us."

"I should not remember it so much without reminder."

"You spoke of it yourself."

"Yes, I should have known there was no need."

"Ah, the weight of years!" said Rhoda. "The weight of understanding, of knowledge! The one does not come without the other. It is all or nothing."

"I have known understanding without years," said Julia. "If I did not say so, I should be an ungrateful mother."

"I have known too much of it," said Fanny. "I am terrified of people's penetration."

"It sounds as if you had no good qualities," said Rhoda. "Or as if no qualities were good."

"Those that incur penetration seldom are. If they were, they would not invite it."

"This is cynical talk," said Julia, smiling.

"I am glad," said Fanny. "I tried to make it so."

"Why do you like to be cynical?" said her sister. "Why not choose some other quality?"

"Because cynicism seems clever. And I think it often is."

"Why do we want to be clever?"

"Oh, I think we must want that. And I think we ought. It is good for other people, better than for ourselves."

"For ourselves it is too much strain," said Walter. "I wish it was natural to me."

"It would be an improvement," said Simon, laughing. "We can often detect the effort."

"That hardly seems a necessary speech," said Sir Edwin.

"We must take it as a brotherly one," said Julia.

"Why is he not content with ordinary intelligence, as I am?"

"Because it is ordinary," said Walter. "I am not as unusual as that."

"Then I suppose I am the unusual one."

"You are in some ways, my boy," said his mother.

"Walter almost says openly that he is clever."

"We must have some way of almost saying it," said Fanny. "We are not allowed to say it quite."

"Surely we do not all think we are clever," said Julia.

"Many of us in one way or another," said Sir Edwin. "Is there anyone here who does not?"

"Well, some kinds of cleverness may help us," said Rhoda. "And we may need the help. To be wiser and kinder. To others and ourselves."

"I could not be kinder to myself than I am," said her sister.

"That may show a knowledge of kindness. It is better that it should be there."

"How far do we understand it?" said Sir Edwin. "A little meets too much gratitude. And much does not meet enough."

"It puts people in too humble a place," said Fanny. "It is not altogether kind."

"Ah, we have to be generous to be grateful," said Rhoda. "One has oneself to be a giver."

"Dinner is ready, ma'am," said Deakin, to Julia.

"So Deakin has learned his lesson," said Simon.

74

"He has not had one to learn," said Rhoda. "Unless it was to learn that."

Simon lingered behind with her, as the others passed.

"You cannot be so much of a giver. You must exist of yourself. This will serve as a beginning. But your nature remains your own. It must assert itself in time."

"I am not here to be myself. I am here for the nearness to your uncle, the power to serve him. That is how I think of his claim on me."

"Some women have seen him in that way. More would have, if he had known more. But he has wanted no one but his brother, offered little to anyone else. I have no great affection for him. It somehow seems a case for truth. I am myself dependent on a brother, but we can look outside ourselves. I welcome you and your sister into our life. And I am a better person than is thought. My habit of not editing myself has its own snare. You will have time to yourself. I hope I may share it?"

"You may have what is over from Edwin. It will give me a purpose for it. But I do not see him as you do. To me he is fitly austere and aloof. But you are right in one thing about him. He asks only for what he can use. I would not give him what is of no good. I would not have him contrive a need. I shall have something to share."

"You have begun to talk in low tones," said Walter, looking back. "That might be a good thing, if overhearing were not better."

"The last is never wise," said Julia. "We none of us talk to people as we do behind their backs."

"Ah, saying things then! It has a poor name," said Rhoda.

"And it is easy to see how it got it," said Fanny, "and how it keeps it. Someone has heard what is said."

"Some people are described in the same way to themselves and other people," said Simon.

"I cannot think of a case," said Fanny.

"What about Simon himself?" said Julia.

"He had come to my mind," said Rhoda. "What more could be said of anyone?"

"Suppose we described ourselves to our faces!" said Fanny.

"Surely we do," said her sister. "We live up to our idea of ourselves."

"I should have thought we were afraid of living according to it."

"You are silent, Uncle," said Simon.

"Well, the talk is an exercise of wits, and mine are getting slow. But I listen to it."

"You talk as if you were eighty, Uncle."

"I talk as if I were seventy, which I am. And I think you do not underestimate it."

"Ah, the time of fulfilment," said Rhoda, "the time of harvest! When the sheaves are gathered, and have not begun to fade!"

"I suppose fading really begins at about forty," said Simon.

"Then I have suffered thirty years of it," said Sir Edwin.

"And I have suffered twelve," said Julia.

"I was not thinking of either of you."

"Perhaps you should have been, my son, as we were involved in what you said."

"Do we think about age more than most people?" said Walter.

"Surely Simon does," said Julia.

"Everyone thinks about it as much as possible," said Simon. "What concerns anyone so much as the time he has to live?"

"Well, when that is over, nothing will concern him," said Sir Edwin.

"To young people the future is still long," said Rhoda.

"Young people forget the gains of experience," said Julia. "If we went back to youth, we should give up a great deal."

"What would it be?" said Simon. "What exactly are the gains?"

"An insight into motive," said Sir Edwin, "a habit of expecting little, an estimate of what is much. Acceptance of fading away, and of other people's acceptance of it."

"I should not mind giving up most of that," said Fanny.

"It is an advance towards the truth," said Rhoda.

"Does it bear out the theory that beauty is truth?" said Walter. "What do you think, Deakin?"

"Well, not only beauty emerges as truth, sir, when you deal with those beneath you."

"We are not supposed to see people in that way."

"I do not know how we can shut our eyes to it, sir, when we have to contend with the difference."

"We must not look down on our fellow-creatures," said Julia.

"We can hardly avoid it in some cases, ma'am, if we look at them at all. The level involves it."

"Ah, to know all is to forgive all," said Rhoda.

"I confess I have not found it so, my lady. To forgive, it is best to know as little as possible."

"Well, my day is ended," said Sir Edwin. "And, Julia, yours should be. You are looking tired."

"I will walk home with Fanny," said Walter, "and prevent Simon from doing so. I must hear what she says about you all."

"Well, you see what we are," said Simon to Rhoda, "what we do and say, what you have before you. I will give you any help I can. I fear it will not be much."

"I may need what it is. If I do, I will ask and take it."

# CHAPTER VI

"THERE IS SOMETHING I must say to you, Walter," said Simon. "And you will hear me in silence. You will not betray any feeling. You will not utter a word to exhibit yourself. You will make neither sign nor sound."

Walter laid a hand on his lips and lifted his eyes to his brother's. But there was a change on his face.

"Rhoda is going to have a child. And I am its father."

There was a silence.

"Could it be Uncle's?" said Walter.

"No. They have not led a married life."

"Could they begin to lead one in time?"

"No. There is no question of it. And things have gone too far."

"How did it come about?"

"You cannot need me to tell you."

"When is it to be?"

"In a few months. It must soon be known."

"Does anyone know yet?"

"No one but you. My uncle does not know. My mother does not. It is all before me."

"We are in trouble, Simon. That is, as you are, I am. Do you want me to break it to Uncle?"

"I want to postpone his knowing. I do not dare to face it. I have hardly faced the truth that he must know."

"Why did you not tell me before?"

"Should we have run with the news? I put it off, as Rhoda put off telling me."

"I don't understand it, Simon. She is so much older than you. She is bound to Uncle in every sense."

"You know that reason has played no part. Would it have happened, if it had?"

"Shall you leave Uncle to find out for himself?"

"You know what I shall do. I shall have to tell him, as I have told you. I cannot leave it to her. I could not have her forced to that. And how will he find out? He will not notice or think of it. He is what he is."

"But that may not be what you think. You may not have to tell him. He may speak himself."

Walter knew better than Simon. It was soon after this that Sir Edwin came to his wife, and spoke with his eyes held from her face.

"I suppose it is Simon?" he said.

Rhoda looked up at him with locked hands.

"No, not Simon. Not by himself. Both of us, neither of us. I do not know what to say. It was fate, impulse, force. What can I say or hope?"

"You have said nothing, except that it is Simon."

"Yes, in the sense you mean."

"We are thinking of no other sense."

"I must ask, Edwin. To think that I must! What is to be done?"

"I can give no answer. If you can tell me anything, I will hear."

"What do you think of us? What can it be?"

"What you know it is. I need not use words that are not mine."

"What is to happen in the end?"

"We do not know what the end will be."

"The other word, Edwin! The word that must be said! What of the child?"

"I shall be the legal father. Nothing else would serve you or me. I must accept the place."

"Are we to tell the truth?"

"To no one. We are both the worse, if it is told. I have no doubt that Walter knows."

"Is Julia to believe the child is yours?"

"She is to accept it as such. We can say no more."

"I must say it once. I know you do not want to hear. How you are yourself!"

"Silence is best also for me."

"Your feeling for me? It must be changed."

"Yes, and my conception of you. I will not say to you what you would not believe."

"It alters my conception of myself."

"It reveals to you what it should be, if you have not known."

"That is a hard word, Edwin."

"What words would you expect from me?"

"What will you say to Simon?"

"Nothing. I will await what he says to me."

Sir Edwin waited without word or sign. And at last the tension and passing time drove Simon to speak. He rose from his desk at a pause in his work, and faced his uncle.

"Uncle, what am I to say to you?"

Sir Edwin met his eyes at once.

"I will hear what it is."

"I hardly know what words to use."

"You would not ask me to help you."

"Can you not take pity on me?"

"Simon, you are yourself a man."

"I can only say that youth and instinct did their work."

"Our instincts are subject to us. That is saying nothing."

"There is nothing I can say," muttered Simon, and said no more.

After this the uncle and nephew went their accustomed way, with Sir Edwin behaving as usual, and Simon doing the same under the general eye. Some weeks later Julia spoke at the table.

"We may see the truth, Edwin, and congratulate you on it? It has been like you not to speak of it. But the time is past."

"Well, you have broken the silence."

"We can think how pleased Hamish would have been."

"Would he have? It would have severed my life from his."

"Surely nothing could have done that."

"It is said that such things do."

"I wish you were more uplifted about it. I may say it of you both."

"Many people might be more so. Perhaps it was hardly thus, that we saw our lives."

"Rhoda, you will come to be glad. I speak to you as a mother. Even now you would not have it otherwise."

"I have hardly thought. It is new to me. I have not had your life, your knowledge. I shall learn from you."

"Have not my nephews their word?" said Sir Edwin, conveying to these that they should do their part.

"It is an event to silence us," said Walter. "No word of ours would count."

Sir Edwin gave him a glance and said no more.

Julia waited until she was alone with her sons.

"Must we suppose that the child is unwanted, that they are so unnatural about it?"

"I think we must suppose it," said Walter.

"What do you think, Simon?"

"That is the impression they give."

"They will adapt themselves. It is the thing that happens. We need have no doubt."

Julia spoke more truth than she knew. Sir Edwin and Rhoda accepted their future, forced to it by the ignorance of others. Rhoda and Simon hardly met or spoke, knowing their relation must fade into a memory. Simon turned to Fanny and his brother for companionship.

At the natural time, with no delay or trouble, a boy was born. And a few days later Sir Edwin spoke to his nephew.

"You have to face the future, Simon. It is in your mind. It is what you have said to yourself. You are no longer to come after me. It is a change for you at your age. It could never be an easy one. There is no help for it. And you can ask no help."

Simon looked at his uncle with startled eyes.

"But—but the boy is mine, Uncle. You and I know it,

though others do not. We can only abide by our knowledge."

"What you and I know is forgotten. The real truth is not the truth to us. We abide by the accepted word."

"But I cannot come after my own son. It is against nature and reason."

"You come after mine."

"But the place is not entailed, Uncle. You can bequeath it as you will. You would not make such a change. It would not be natural or fit. You will provide for the boy in another way, on another scale. Or I will provide for him. It is the only thing."

"It is a thing that could not be. Think what you say. Think of him as he is thought of. Think of his place. He is to be always with me. All that I have is his. It is natural, inevitable, rooted in the past. Do you mean you have not thought of it?"

"I did not imagine you seeing him as your son. Your dealing with me as a culprit hardly supports it."

"How else should I deal with you? But we have to veil the truth. I will accept no reproach from you. That is on the other side. I am not an agent in the matter. I need hardly be brought into it. No one need give a thought to me. No one has done so."

"You must have your own feeling towards the change."

"Your son would have come after you. Now he takes your place. It is only a foreshortening of the future, a cutting out of your life."

"But my life is before me. What is it to be?"

"You expect me to give my mind to it? What is your reason? What should be mine?"

"Uncle, it was the instinct of a moment. I was not master of myself. I meant to do harm to no one. You must understand."

"I do not. I have been my own master."

"Your temptations have been different. Such as they were, you have yielded to them. You have lived aloof and for yourself. You failed in courage under grief. Your marriage is part of the failure. You have met tolerance from me. And you should remember that I have served you."

"In serving your future. I do not forget. You have been open about it."

"I must ask you again, Uncle. What is my life to be? I shall have to live it."

"Have you thought what is to be mine? Yours is not a thing by itself. I have also to live, though you have hardly accepted it."

Simon stood in silence, seeming not to know he did so. Then he spoke with a difference.

"It must be as it must, Uncle. I wonder with you that I have not seen it. I was too sunk in my own life to reason. I can only confess it and put my mistake behind."

"And what do you see in front?"

"What other men see. It is time I saw it. I must steer my own course, find work to serve myself and others. I will work for you here until you fill my place."

"For me and not with me?" said Sir Edwin, almost with a smile. "Perhaps I need not fill it. It will be many years before my son—yes, that is what he is—is old enough to take it. He may never be suited to it. He may never wish to. The estate can carry the post, though the prospect must be different. It would solve your problem, and keep you together as a family."

There was another silence.

"I accept the offer, Uncle. I should thank you for it. I have brought the change on myself. Without will or purpose, but by no fault of anyone else. I must face it as retribution. But what if I marry?"

"With your mother's help you should be able. You will be glad that the boy is known as mine. We must have forgotten that he is not. He will send a difference through many lives. One should come at once. It will be best for you and your mother to leave this house."

"For what reason, Uncle? I see there may be many."

"When I die—and you realise I shall do so—my wife will be its mistress until her son's marriage. As he grows up, he will expect it. She can no longer take matters into her own hands. And if you marry, a second family can hardly be here. It will be well to make the change."

"I should have seen it, Uncle. But I have thought of things as established. They had always been as they were. My place will never be here again. As you say, it is a change through many lives."

"It is a change through yours. And through mine in another degree. Your mother and I have talked of it. She saw what would be involved in my having a son. And she could not know I should have no other children. She did not speak of it to you, fearing to touch on a point that might be a sore one. But she assumed your thoughts were working on the same line."

"I had better support the theory. She could hardly think anything else. I cannot explain that I was misled by the sense of my fatherhood. I see how simple I have been. She says I am in some ways simpler than other men. But I am not a man who must live a life based on inheritance. I should be ashamed to be."

"You must discuss things with your mother. Her income will help you, as it has helped me. I shall face a certain straitness. But things should be possible for us all."

"What is the boy to be called, Uncle?"

"Hamish," said Sir Edwin, just glancing at his nephew's face.

"I wonder at that. Though it bears out the supposed truth."

"So you do not wonder at it. No one else will do so."

"Uncle, may I ask you something once? Are you glad at all to be thought to have a son?"

"It is like you to ask it," said Sir Edwin, and gave no answer.

84

Simon went to the room where his mother and brother were alone.

"I have had my talk with my uncle, and settled my fate. I am to continue my work here, on another basis. And we are to leave this house, we must suppose never to return. His wife is its mistress, as the mother of the heir. Nothing else would lead to the future. I am a humbler person, displaced, deposed. But I can make the best of it."

"So am I," said Julia. "And I can do the same. My son, I have not spoken of it. You were making the transition in your mind. I knew it was a hard and sad one."

Simon was silent, seeing how his abstraction had been explained.

"I look up to you both," said Walter. "I wish I could suffer something, so that I could quietly rise above it."

"Your poetic talent may desert you," said Simon, trying to be himself.

"No, it is a part of me."

"As this house seemed of me," said Simon, looking round. "Well, I am to leave it and lose it. And so are you, Mater, after as long a time. But it has not been so much your own."

"As something of yours, my son, it has been mine. I have thought of you more than of myself."

"So have I," said Walter. "And that means a great deal of thought. I have shared the suspense that is worse than certainty. And I hardly think it is."

Simon said nothing. His blindness to his coming displacement was the only error he never confessed to his brother.

"We shall have to find a house," said Julia; "and one on the place, as you are to manage it. I cannot think of one."

"There is Fanny's house," said Simon. "I do not know of another. Would it be well for me to marry her, and for all of us to live in it? It is fully large."

"And it is good to have some reason for marrying," said Walter.

"Simon, nothing will alter you," said Julia. "You are more and more yourself."

"Fanny would not want an emotional married life. She was not responsive with her sister. Marriages are arranged in other countries, and are often a success. They have a better basis than a passing emotion. I could get attached to Fanny, and I should make her a good husband."

"Are we to consider her feeling for you?"

"Mater, you said that Simon was himself," said Walter "You must not be surprised by his being so."

"She is lonely and unsettled," said Simon. "She has no great feeling for anyone. It would make a better life for her. And I would say she had an affection for me, if I should not be accused of being myself."

"For the moment you might almost be someone else," said his brother.

"So I am to live as a member of her household, after being the mistress of this," said Julia. "I said I thought of you more than of myself. I wonder if I can go on doing so."

"You might manage the house, as your income is larger than Fanny's. I daresay she would not mind."

"I might not, and would not. I will order no other home that is not my own. And I should have no respect for her, if she did not mind. She would have no self-respect. Both things were really true in the other case."

"I should have a particular respect for her," said Walter. "I do not know what you mean."

"Then you had one for Rhoda," said his mother.

"I had. But somehow I lost it. I cannot give a reason."

"You mean you will not. And I do not need one. We are saying the same thing."

"When people do that, they always say such different things."

"I mean no more than that people should fill their own place."

"Well, they will do so," said Simon. "But I think losing it imposes a greater strain."

86

"I wonder if your uncle will have any more children," said Julia.

"I do not think so. He and Rhoda are hardly on those terms."

"That is what we thought. But we have had to think again. What would your father say to the course of things?"

"What would anyone say to what happens after his death? What happened before we lived, seems strange enough."

"It is only when we are alive that things are normal," said Walter. "It shows how important our presence is."

"I wonder what they will call the boy," said Julia.

"Hamish," said Simon. "My uncle told me."

"So you have been having some chat with him," said Walter. "I somehow cannot imagine it."

"He may feel some remorse towards you," said Julia. "He has caused this change in your life. He should be grateful for the way you accept it. But when I spoke of you, he did not respond. I thought it was grudging of him. You are his brother's son, and his brother has been the first person in his life."

"And I think will remain so," said Simon.

"He may get a strong feeling for his own son."

"I think it will never be as strong."

"You seem to be in his confidence, as we are not. I should not have expected it. It may be a sign of his compunction."

"I do not think it is."

"Well, perhaps you understand each other."

"I understand his feeling at the moment."

"It is good of you to try to, my boy."

"It does not need much effort."

"Well, can you explain his aloofness? We have tried to show him sympathy."

"His life is strange to him. He is not of an age to adapt himself."

"It has turned out to his advantage. It gives him a stake

in the future. Well, I must go and see his wife and son. You will both see them later."

"That should have been in a play," said Walter. "With the audience knowing the truth."

"Well, it was, with you as audience."

"I felt too much involved in it. I found it a perilous passage. I suppose there will be many."

"Until we have forgotten the truth. We must see that we forget it."

"I must ask it once, Simon. How will you feel to the boy?"

"I will answer it once. I feel I am giving him my place. It is a reasonless feeling, but I have it. And he will have a father."

"How will it be, as time goes on?"

"I shall watch him with personal feeling. But in the end I shall be in thrall to him. I shall have my deserts, and hardly proportionate ones. It must make its difference."

"How will you feel to Rhoda?"

"We shall become more distant. We have done so. Under my uncle's eye what else could be? And she may be my sister-in-law."

"I suppose you will take steps to bring that about."

Simon did so, and a week or two later led Fanny to his mother.

"Mater, you have wished for a daughter. Here I bring one to you. I told you my hopes. Now I have the better thing to tell."

"My reproach is taken away," said Walter. "I am justified in being what I am."

"I have felt as Simon says," said Julia. "Now my future opens in my daughter's house. I shall not be without a refuge, as I grow old. She shall not be without a mother."

"What will your uncle say to it, Simon?" said Fanny.

"He can only give his consent. His feeling will not be strong. He has little affection for me. We have little for each other. He could not forgive my realising that I should

88

come after him. But now that is in the past, we may understand each other better."

"Or forget you ever understood each other. That is what that usually means."

"It was terrible to see their understanding," said Walter. "Simon knew Uncle had to die, and did not disguise it."

"Well, now he has to live," said Fanny. "And anyhow he is going to."

"I could not profess to think he was immortal," said Simon.

"People cannot suffer our picturing things without them."

"A man of seventy could hardly feel in that way."

"You don't know how people feel. The old do not think how good it is to be young. They pity the young for not being what they are themselves. And the pity is real."

"So everyone pities everyone else," said Julia. "And I daresay with reason. Life can be a sorry thing."

"That is true," said Sir Edwin, entering the room. "But it responds in a measure to ourselves. I used to wonder if the difference in us would give out. But it never did."

"What do you think, Deakin?" said Simon.

"As Sir Edwin does, sir. I am confronted by the lack of standard."

"What do you say to the changes? No doubt you know of them."

"It is for me to accept them, sir."

"You will miss the mistress. You think of my mother as that."

Deakin moved about his duties without reply.

"I daresay you would come with us. But you are above our level."

"Deakin belongs to the house," said Sir Edwin, easily. "You force us to your level, Simon."

"Yes, Sir Edwin. Man and boy I have belonged to it."

"And I come from outside," said Julia. "I have no place."

"It is what the lady must do, ma'am," said Deakin.

"I am to hang up my hat in my wife's hall," said Simon.

"No, you are not," said Fanny. "The house will depend on your support. I can barely struggle along in it. And I shall rely on your mother and not acknowledge it."

"What a change it all is! We must wonder what my father would say to it."

"So in your place you do so," said Sir Edwin. "In mine I know what he would say."

"He will always be first to you, Uncle."

Sir Edwin made no reply.

"Your son is so healthy and contented, Edwin," said Julia. "He reminds me of Simon at his age."

"They are first cousins," said Fanny. "They are often more alike than brothers."

"He might have been like Walter. But he makes me think of Simon. His eyes are set in the same way. I shall like to watch him grow up. He somehow seems nearer to me than a nephew by marriage."

"You may catch a likeness to Hamish," said Sir Edwin. "That would not be unnatural."

"I am glad he is to have his name, Edwin. It carries on the meaning of your lives."

"You might have wanted the name for your own grandson."

"He can have another," said Simon. "But I hope I shall have a daughter. There is nothing for a son to inherit, and a girl means more to a father."

"There is only this child between you and the place," said Sir Edwin. "But it is not a line for your thought."

"Yes, of course you will have no other children. But I do not know why I should say that."

"No one can know why you say anything, Simon," said Julia.

"If we have a child, it will be a first cousin to this one," said Fanny. "And another cousin through you and your uncle."

"Yes, they would be doubly related. A marriage would not be possible."

"It would be legally so, but perhaps not desirable," said Julia.

"It could not be allowed," said Simon. "But the question is not urgent."

"It is idle to plan the future. It is not in our hands. It may grow out of our actions."

"Those are often hardly deliberate."

"I hope not often," said Sir Edwin. "We have reason, and should be governed by it."

"What do you think, Deakin?" said Walter.

"I have found that people may be governed by other things, sir."

"Lower things, you mean?"

"Well, sir, it is hard not to use the word."

"Well, I must go home," said Fanny. "To the house that will soon be that to me again."

"I will come with you," said Julia, "and talk of what has to be done. It is to be home to me as well."

There was a minute of silence when the three men were alone.

"It was like a Greek tragedy," said Walter. "With people saying things with a meaning they did not know, or with more meaning than they knew. It was not the first to-day. Will it always be like this?"

"It must not be," said his uncle. "We are to forget the truth. It must not lie below the surface, ready to escape. It is strange enough, Simon, that you are the person whom we doubt."

"You can hardly do so, Uncle. You know what I have at stake. What would be the cost to me, if the truth were known? In itself it has cost me enough."

Sir Edwin left the room, and Walter turned to his brother.

"What kind of a man is our uncle?"

"He is no better than you or I. It is best for himself that

the truth should be hidden. If it emerged, his dignity would suffer, a thing he has never faced. And he could hardly wish me to lose any more. I have lost enough. And I have done him no deliberate harm."

"You must have made love to his wife."

"If there are to be no more words, let there be none."

"Tell me once what you feel about everything, Simon. Somehow it is hard to know."

"I can put it in a word. The place is the thing I love. Above any man or woman, above you yourself, above all else. And I am cast from it, and shall see it pass further away. My feelings are dulled. You ask me what they are. To myself I seem to have none."

# CHAPTER VII

"Dɪᴅ ʏᴏᴜ ɴᴏᴛ see your mother come into the room?" said Simon.

His son rose to his feet, glancing with a half-smile at his sister.

"And do not exchange glances with Naomi. You are too old to be so mannerless."

"Eighteen years is hardly past youth," said his daughter.

"I shall be going in and out," said Fanny. "I have some things to arrange."

"Then I must behave like a Jack-in-the-box," said her son.

"The deportment required of you," said his brother.

"And of you," said Simon. "You may take what I said, to yourself."

"Simon, is there any need to be so sour and sharp?" said Julia, in a tone that seemed to illustrate her words.

"I will not see my sons become boors. We can afford them no training and must act as mentors ourselves. It is not a choice I would have made. I am not cut out for the character. But certain things are forced upon me."

"Do you think you and Walter were better at their age?"

"We had another background. They are more dependent on their parents. It is no kindness to fail them."

"It is not always clear where kindness lies."

"I suppose it is real kindness," said Ralph. "That does lie in unexpected ways."

"Do not copy your uncle," said Simon. "Whatever you can or cannot be, you can be yourself."

"But that is the trouble, Father," said Naomi. "They have to be someone else."

"I like to be copied," said Walter. "It is a proof of what

I have been. I hope people will not forget who was the original."

"Must you stand about in that conscious way?" said Simon, to his sons. "There are surely chairs in the room."

"Mother is coming in and out, sir," said Graham. "It is the line of least resistance."

"What is that to do with it? Are you at a stage when energy fails?"

"I am sorry to disturb you, Mrs. Challoner," said a lady at the door, looking from Fanny to Julia, as if hardly distinguishing between the owners of the name. "But now that Naomi is seventeen, should she go with her brothers to their tutor? It hardly seems a proper thing."

"But he teaches subjects you do not, Miss Dolton," said Simon, mildly. "And it is better that she should learn them."

"I have never felt the want of them, Mr. Challoner."

Simon was at a loss, and Naomi checked a laugh without full success.

"Things are different since your day—our day, Miss Dolton," said Julia.

"I know I am not entirely up to date, Mrs. Challoner."

"That is not what I said. I meant to support my son."

"Then what did she say?" murmured Naomi.

Miss Dolton was a hurried-looking woman, who had come to the house as nursery governess, and remained to organise an upstairs life for pupils grown beyond her. Simon did not countenance his children's presence at his board.

"You can take proper care of your sister," he said. "I hope I need not say it. And when you get to your books, forget yourselves and attend to them. The one thing between you and the workhouse is your education, such as it is. I imagine you do not want to end in it."

"I think we must do so, sir," said Graham. "We could hardly provide for our old age. The question is how much of our life we can spend out of it."

"Well, it rests with you. Your chances are up to the average. And most people avoid it."

"Did you have a good breakfast?" said Fanny to her children. "It is a chilly day."

"We had what was provided," said Ralph. "I should perhaps hardly use your word."

"Surely it was enough?"

"It is not quantity that fails. It may not be the right preparation for the workhouse, that we do not have to ask for more."

"Do not be so childish," said Simon. "What talk for a boy of fifteen! In another class you might be earning your bread."

"I wonder how long we shall have it provided," said Graham, when they had saluted their parents and withdrawn.

"As long as we have it with Miss Dolton," said Naomi. "We could not afford the arrangement ourselves. It is an expense to Father to keep us below him."

The brothers and sister left the house, Graham and Naomi resembling Simon, but slighter in form and feature; and Ralph as much like his mother as a boy could be to a woman. They accepted their life as the one they lived, and the one they shared, with a humour that modified its harm.

"Simon, things are too much for you," said Julia. "You are so seldom your real self. We are in danger of forgetting what it was."

"Things fall heavy on me, Mater, and must do so. My work for my uncle, the poor return, the headship of my family, the knowledge that I take your income, burden my wife, and am a cross-grained, middle-aged man before my time! I was not brought up to this way of life. My early years did not fit me for it. My sons are happier in looking to a future that will be theirs."

"I almost wish you could forget those years. So far from being a happy memory, they feed your disappointment. It

95

was a great and sudden one, but it is in the past. It seems it might be buried with it."

"It goes through the present and the future. It will be with me in old age, when memories are clear. I do not want to complain, but I am pursued by it. And other people suffer with me."

"Why do what you do not want to?" said Fanny. "We are none of us the better for it."

"I think I am," said Walter. "I am fascinated by people's troubles, when they are not sickness or death. I never tire of them, even in my own family, though I would rather they were somewhere else."

"Sickness of heart and the death of hope," said Simon, with a grim smile. "Do they serve your purpose?"

"It is making too much of it," said Julia. "You have a great deal in your life. I cannot understand your not seeing it."

"Mrs. Challoner," said Miss Dolton, at the door, "Nurse has come to me in some trouble. Claud has not eaten his breakfast, and has ended by throwing it on the carpet."

"Why have a carpet in the nursery?" said Simon. "Surely there are things that wash."

"It is worn drugget," said Miss Dolton, with a faint sigh. "And Emma was just prevented from doing the same. She always tries to copy him."

"Then if we see he is well educated and conducted, we shall kill two birds with one stone," said Fanny.

Miss Dolton turned to the door, whose handle was being agitated by an unpractised hand, and Simon's third son entered.

"Very naughty boy," he observed, looking at Julia, to whose judgement he inclined.

"Yes, that is what you have been."

"Emma very good girl," said Claud, without expression.

"Yes, she does not throw things on the floor. You are too old to do that."

"Five, six," said Claud, in allusion to his own age.

"He is just three," said Miss Dolton, taking his hand.

"Emma only two," said Claud, and submitted to be led away.

"The twelve years between the two youngest boys will make problems," said Fanny.

"Imagine the blank filled," said Walter. "And then think what they would be."

The door again opened.

"I am sorry, Mrs. Challoner, but Emma insists on coming in. She knows Claud has done so."

"Unny," said Simon's second daughter, advancing into the room.

"She wants some bread and honey from our table," said Fanny.

"It is sticky," said Miss Dolton, and said no more.

"No!" said Emma, with threat in her tone.

"I will make her a sandwich," said Julia.

Emma watched the proceeding with concentration, took the sandwich with her eyes on it, and turned away.

"What do you say?" said Miss Dolton.

"No," said Emma, in repudiation of formality.

"Whom do you love?" said Fanny, taking her up.

"Nurse," said Emma, her eyes on the sandwich.

"But you love your mother too?"

"No," said Emma, absently.

"Not even a little bit?"

"No," said Emma, and looked at Miss Dolton, in anticipation of release.

"I must go to my uncle," said Simon. "He grows more exacting with every hour. Of course he is nearly eighty-nine."

"So you would not yet have been in his place, if he had not married," said Julia.

"But in a different one of my own. That does not alter what I have said."

"It is a pity it does not," said Fanny. "We can only wish something would."

97

"I must sometimes say a word of myself in my own house. People must realise that I exist. They tend to forget it."

"Who does so? Your elder children?"

"You mean they are not at ease with me. That is a thing that cannot be helped. I was not so with my own father. And they should not be too much."

"I am not so sure," said Julia. "They might do better under less constraint."

"They might do nothing. That is the danger. I am grateful for the compulsions of my boyhood."

"I am not," said Walter. "They rise up before me in the night. I might have been a less bitter poet without them."

"People do expect eventual gratitude for early rigour," said Fanny. "Only the opposite has aroused my own."

"We will both face our deserts," said Simon. "I shall not flinch before mine."

"Your boys are young to begin calling you 'sir', Simon," said Julia. "You never called your own father that."

"It would have been as well if we had. All that 'Father' and 'Uncle' was effeminate. We were not daughters."

"I wonder what made them think of it."

"Their address of their tutor," said Walter. "Another distant and authoritative male. I wonder how they dared to begin it. I suppose they could not any longer see Simon as a father."

"Why do they never say good-bye to me?" said Julia, in a neutral tone.

"These unwritten laws grow up in families," said Fanny. "They honour their father and their mother. Anything further would weaken it."

"They shall do so to you, if you wish, Mater," said Simon.

"No, I only value spontaneous remembrance."

"What if we could see into our children's minds?" said Fanny.

"It would confirm the wisdom of our course," said

Simon. "Their criticism would point to their own need of it."

"They might say the same to you. Let us suppose we could hear them talk."

"I can imagine Naomi taking the lead there."

Naomi was walking in silence between her brothers, who were also silent. It was their habit to go in this way from their father's presence. When they approached their great-uncle's gate, a tall youth was standing by it, a plainer, etherealised copy of Simon at his age, and resembling Naomi and Graham.

"Good day to you," he said with a smile. "I knew you would be passing. I came out to have a word with you before breakfast."

"In our case it will be after it," said Graham. "Miss Dolton has presided at ours and released us."

"Yes, I remember you do not have meals with your parents."

"We do nothing that would imply equality with them. We live in organised rigour two floors above."

"What is the reason?" said Hamish, gently.

"To spare them our presence. And prepare us for the workhouse by accustoming us to its standard."

"We are content to be ourselves," said Naomi. "But being treated as what you are is different. Most of us are treated as if no one knew it."

"And so can assume that no one does know," said Graham.

"I hardly know what I am," said Hamish.

"We can tell you," said Ralph. "The son of the head of the family, and its future head."

"We cannot foretell the future."

"My father can. He foretold it again this morning. For us it remains as we said."

"He seems to resent our prospect for us," said Naomi. "And he should be grateful for a provision for us, that he cannot make himself."

"I wonder why he thinks we shall be welcome," said Graham. "It is not his usual view of us."

"I have heard that the workhouse conditions are being improved," said Hamish, smiling.

"I hardly think he can have heard," said Graham. "Or it might not serve as our destiny."

"It might suggest a higher standard on our floor," said Naomi. "There seems to be an assumed correspondence with it."

"I should hardly have thought your house was large enough for life on separate floors."

"It is not," said Naomi. "That may be why it is used for it. The workhouse is probably not large enough for the number of its inmates."

"Where do the little ones live? I suppose on a still higher floor. I did the same at their age. Now I am with my parents. My father is eighty-nine to-day."

"Wish him many happy returns of the day for us," said Graham. "He will expect it the more for having got so used to it."

"I have wished them for myself. And he did not seem surprised."

"You will soon be the head of things," said Ralph "It would be my father's prospect, if you had not been born. Perhaps he did not mean us to be of so little account."

"Or meant only us to be," said Naomi. "Now he has almost become so himself."

"I should not have said so," said Graham. "Either of him or Grandmamma. Sometimes I am afraid for Mother."

"There is something in her that prevents it," said Ralph.

"I hope there is indeed. It would be terrible for your mother to be so. Think what it would suggest about yourself! And Father would not be blind to it."

"There is nothing in us to prevent it," said Naomi. "Or if there was, it has been forced out of us. That is what underlies our training, that there might have been something in us to begin with like that."

"It sounds as if your training may have been wasted," said Hamish.

"It has been. It has made us feel we can rise above it. And if we feel we could be above anything, it is wasted indeed."

"I suppose I have had no training."

"Unless you give the name to Eton and Oxford," said Graham.

"I do not. There is no comparison."

"No, they lead you to think that things are due to you. And no one needs any training to think that."

"Well, I must say good-bye. I should like to be coming with you."

"Do not forget to say to your father for us: 'O Great-uncle, live for ever.'"

"I will say it for you. And he does his best to obey."

"Why is Hamish the pathetic one amongst us?" said Naomi, as they went on. "Perhaps the pathos is too settled in our case to count."

"He is rich and can hardly enter the kingdom of heaven," said Graham. "And by nature he belongs to it. Our true place is outside."

"I should wish he was our brother, if I felt he could support being Father's son."

"Father is better to him than to us," said Ralph. "But it may be because he is better than we are."

"He ought to be," said Graham. "We give back what we are given. We can hardly be high in the human scale."

"Father can't help being poor," said Naomi. "It is clear that he would not have chosen it. That is why we are guilty in depending on him. It can only make him poorer."

"It is Hamish who has deprived him of his heritage. He is always more at home in the other house. He still feels he is in exile. When he is there, we can see the difference it has made to him."

They were to see something of this to-day. When they

returned from their tutor, Hamish was again at the gate.

"I am to ask you all in to luncheon, to celebrate my father's birthday. Our elders are in the house. He is happy in the thought of having you, and my mother is almost happier. You give us something we are without."

# CHAPTER VIII

"My Fanny, my sister!" said Rhoda. "My little sister and her large family! How they are welcome! Ah, how dear they are! Our empty table will be full. Some of them have had their places there. They are to feel at home."

"Yes, my mother had your place for many years," said Simon. "Even after it was yours."

"She taught me to fill it. How I watched her there! It was a lesson I do not forget."

"I always think of my father in this house."

"As is natural," said Sir Edwin. "He was here until you were a man."

"Ah, the other Hamish!" said Rhoda. "How he is with us! How he is in our lives! How he will live to the end of them! My Hamish knows there is an example for him in our hearts."

"Your Hamish is more like Simon," said Julia. "They always remind me of each other. Especially when they are tired or ill. Not that they are often either."

"Hamish does seem rather sick at heart," said Graham to his sister. "And for that matter so does Father."

"What did you say?" said Simon.

"Oh, nothing, sir. It was nothing that mattered."

"I throw no doubt on it. But you will not mutter at this table. What was your reason for doing so?"

"I thought perhaps my voice should not be heard."

"Then let it not be. You know the way to avoid it."

"I wish no guest to be silent at my table," said Sir Edwin. "I am grateful to those who celebrate my living another year beyond my span. It is kind to appear to be glad of it."

"And how easy that is!" said his wife. "How good a thing it is to us! In itself how good a thing!"

"So what did you say, Graham?" said Sir Edwin.

"It is not worth repeating, Uncle."

"We will still ask to hear it."

"I said that Hamish and my father both seemed rather sick at heart."

"They seem to you so? But I wonder you voiced the thought."

"As my father said, I hardly did so. I have been forced to it. I feel some wonder on my side."

"Pray let someone else utter his thoughts," said Simon. "We have heard Graham's."

"Perhaps I am a little sick at heart," said Hamish to Naomi. "More than you are, though you may feel you have more reason. Something is wanting in my life, that is not in yours."

"Do you feel the verdict is true of you, Simon?" said Julia.

"Well, I am often a tired and harassed man."

"Tired you can hardly be," said Sir Edwin. "Your work for me does not warrant it."

"I have other demands on me, Uncle. Some of them are here."

"I refuse to be a demand," said Julia.

"So do I," said Fanny, "though it may be what I am."

"I wonder if I can refuse," said Naomi.

"You can all three do so," said Simon. "A woman has her own rights and makes her own return."

"And neither can be said of us," said Ralph to Graham. "And neither is said."

"Who put you two together?" said his father.

"Aunt Rhoda, I suppose, sir. We were in her hands."

"I will ask her to let you change places with Hamish."

"May I keep my place by Naomi, Cousin Simon?" said the latter. "It is a promise I have made to myself."

"It is Ralph and Graham whom I want to separate. But they can remain where they are, on condition of silence."

"I think they do not merit that," said Julia. "I see no reason."

"They can take it as the outcome of my being sick at heart. That is what I am to them."

"Is Cousin Simon often like this?" said Hamish to Naomi.

"He is always strange, when he is in this house. Either silent or as you see him. He seems to feel he has lost his rights, and to forget they are no longer his. Losing them seems to have torn away a part of him. He is not what he was meant to be."

"I have a strange father in another way. He hardly seems to see me as what I am. His feeling for his brother is the real one in his life. There again a part of him has been torn away. I used to hope I might grow into his heart, as something young and his own. But it was an empty hope. The thing was not to be."

"He has been good to you?" said Naomi.

"Too good. Too considerate and kind for a father to a son. I would have chosen a more natural relation. Yes, I would have chosen yours. But I must take what falls to me."

"What are you discussing so earnestly?" said Julia.

"Fathers and their sons," said Hamish.

"I am glad I am only an uncle," said Walter. "I should not dare to be more."

"The position of a father involves many things," said Simon.

"That of the children also. They confront someone in power."

"It is the young who have that," said Julia.

"So people say," said Graham. "I have no idea on what ground."

"Neither have I," said his father. "Power is for those who have earned it."

"The young have the rights in the future," said Julia.

"But they live in the present," said her grandson. "And they have few there. And the future is not represented as affording many. Indeed only the one."

"I hope our great-uncle is having a happy birthday," said Naomi. "We are here to ensure it, and I suppose this is our best."

"He is the better for having you here," said Hamish. "He seems to miss you, though you have never lived in his house. You are his brother's descendants. He does not see me as apart from you. I am one amongst you, no more to him that you are. I hope I am as much."

"Edwin, you are such a handsome man," said Julia. "Each time I see you, your looks have gained. I wish my Hamish could meet you as you are now. He would have even more to see than he once saw."

"I wish he could. I wish we could meet each other."

"I think Naomi is like her great-uncle," said Simon.

"In a way she is. But his looks are so much his own. I cannot think of anyone equal to him."

"Do you think about your looks, Father?" said Hamish.

"No, I take them for granted. They are of a high order, and remain so. But I would rather say it of other things; of brain or personality or character."

"Ah, how we say it for you!" murmured Ralph, in mimicry of his aunt. "And how we all mean it! Ah, how we do!"

"What did you say, Ralph?" said Simon.

There was a pause.

"Is this a silence that speaks?" said Graham.

"If only it was!" said Naomi. "Or if only something would do so!"

"What did you say, Ralph?" repeated Simon.

"What I might have said, what I am glad has been said," said Rhoda, in easy, fluent tones. "Why should I find fault with it?"

"You know the reasons," said Simon. "It is kind not to give them. The boy is dependent on the kindness, and I am so for him."

"You are my guests, and have a right to it."

"We are what you say, and should not presume on it."

"I don't think your young people lack brains, Simon," said Sir Edwin, continuing from his words, as if he had not heard the last ones.

"Well, I hope they have the character to use them."

"In order to avoid the accepted alternative," said Graham.

"Why do you think it a matter for jest?" said his father. "Poverty is a test few people can stand. You have no idea what it means. Your life is easier than most."

"It is the first time he has told us," said Ralph. "How did he find it out?"

"Hamish does not have to listen to these warnings," said Fanny.

"My Hamish! Ought he to hear them?" said Rhoda, with a glance at Ralph. "No, his mother will not say it."

"He is in no need of them," said Simon. "His future is different."

"The future that was yours, sir," said Hamish. "There was a displacement of the line. I should not have existed."

"Are you glad that you do?"

"I suppose I am. It is a difficult question to answer."

"I should not have thought it. You do not seem to find it so. The answer is the one you give."

"We are all glad," said Fanny.

"My sister! I know you are," said Rhoda. "How glad I am of all your children!"

"Well, I hope you will remain so. I hear some more of them."

"The nurse is here with the little ones, my lady," said Deakin. "They have come to wish Sir Edwin many happy returns."

The guests gave no sign of this or any purpose, as they stood within the door. Claud remained by his nurse, and Emma showed a tendency to vague advance.

"Many happy returns of the day, Great-Uncle," said Julia.

"No," said Emma.

Claud made no response.

"You know it is his birthday."

"Not birthday," said Claud, looking at Sir Edwin, as though something in him precluded such an occasion.

"Poor Uncle Edwin!" said Emma.

"Would you like to live for nearly ninety years?" said their uncle.

"Oh, yes," said Claud.

"But you think I should die, now I have lived for so long?"

"Not die!" said Emma, with emotion.

"Ah, what a stage!" said Rhoda. "How I remember Hamish in it!"

"Dear little girl!" said Emma, in agreement.

"You are not behaving very nicely," said Julia.

"But have it," said Emma, looking at the table and alluding to a system of rewards for doing so.

Claud's eyes followed hers.

"Well, choose something and say good-bye," said Simon.

The guests obeyed the first injunction, passed over the second, and went to the door.

"There will be demands on you in the future, Simon," said Sir Edwin.

"I hope Graham will be off my hands, before Claud comes on to them. The gap in years should help us."

"The workhouse may also benefit," said Graham. "I may be dead before the date of Claud's admittance."

"I forbid any more of that talk," said Simon. "It is becoming a performance. And as such it should entertain."

"You must keep your own rule, Simon," said Julia.

"I am a law to myself. What do you think is my place in the family? The subject was mine, and this travestying of it is senseless. Graham is too old for it."

"For the subject of our final stage?" said Naomi. "We can never get beyond it."

"Have you any alternative ideas for your sons' future, Simon?" said Sir Edwin.

"They will go to Oxford. We have cut out the expense of a public school to ensure it. And some sort of self-support should result from it. Must result, I should say."

"To keep the climax at bay," said Ralph.

"Did you hear what I said?" said his father. "Will this brilliance be put to any purpose, besides hounding one point to death? You cannot afford to waste your talents. There can only be one end to it. And I do not want a boyish joke made out of that. It is a poor sense of humour that must be exercised on family subjects. If it has no general use, it is worth nothing."

"The workhouse is at once granted and grudged its place in the family," said Naomi.

"Edwin, it is good to see you at the head of your table," said Julia. "With Hamish at your side, ready to take your place. If my Hamish could see it, he would be content for his son to yield to yours."

"It is the kinder to say it, that we may doubt its truth. And we should not lay too much stress on being followed by a son. It is no man's right."

"That is how my father feels," said Hamish to Naomi. "I have done little for him by being in his life. If it were not for my mother, I should feel I had no place in it. And I sometimes think she has hardly had what is her due."

"He was an old man when you were born. It was late to make the change."

"He is not old now, except in years. His heart and feelings are alive. And they are fixed on his brother, as they have always been. It is a strange life story. It is for us all a strange, difficult thing."

"We hardly have a place in our father's life. Our empty places are in the home and the life that once were his. It is almost true to say that he does not live."

"Your place is here, always empty to me, always yours. I hope it will not wait too long."

"What are you talking about so gravely?" said Simon.

"About our different homes," said Naomi. "I daresay we should have come to the final one in time."

"Have you a great feeling for your home, Hamish?"

"Not as great as you have, sir. It has not been mine for as long. I have a sense of being an afterthought."

"You will lose the feeling. You should never have had it. I do not know why you have."

"It is no place for me alone. Or even for my mother and me. It seems to be empty, bereft of something, waiting for someone."

"You talk as if you were not a boy, and had never been one."

"My Hamish, my son!" said Rhoda. "He has been more for his mother's sake."

"Do you ever imagine your descendants here, Cousin Simon? You must once have had the picture in your mind."

"I have lost it. I have left my home. I do not look back or think of it. I move forward like any other man."

"Our own home has an unsettled feeling," said Ralph. "It can be seen as a halfway house."

"You can hardly feel that," said Fanny. "It is the only home you have known."

"The ones that come before and after seem to have more claim."

"I must thank you all for coming to honour my birthday," said Sir Edwin. "I am old to make a speech, but I feel and acknowledge the honour. I have the guests I should have chosen, my brother's family. I have been in my place very long. It is soon to know me no more. I thank you who have helped me in it."

"It will always be empty to us, Edwin," said Julia. "Hamish will fill another. And that in its turn will be empty, until memories die."

"What is wrong about lofty words," said Walter, "is that other people have said them. And when I think of some myself, the moment is past."

"Do we really think of them?" said Graham. "Or do we

just feel the impulse? We should not enjoy it so much, if the effort was involved."

"I am ashamed of being young at these moments," said Naomi. "No one can speak greatly except from experience."

"Would you not be ashamed of being as old as Uncle Edwin?" said Ralph, in an undertone. "Of being so soon to die? It seems somehow humbling."

"Of what should she be ashamed?" said Simon. "Speak so that we can hear you."

"I heard him," said Sir Edwin. "It is shameful to be soon to die. Well, I shall not see the future, and I see a shorter past. The place has its lowliness."

"Did you say that, Ralph?"

"No, not really, sir. I asked a question."

"How do you think you chose your time?"

"I did not mean to be heard."

"Have you said before, at the table of someone in old age, that you would be ashamed of being so?"

"I suppose I have not. The question has not arisen. I daresay to be young is just as pitiful."

"If youth leads you to this, it is what you say. I cannot be proud of my sons."

"Nor I of my father," muttered Ralph. "Yes, what did I say, sir? I said I was not proud of you, and I am not."

"What fault do you find with me?"

"You cannot need me to tell you."

"I have asked you to do so."

"You forget you have a duty to us. You forget how you were dealt with yourself. It is not our fault that your life is changed. Our poor outlook is no advantage to us. It is not fair to hold us guilty because of it."

"It will not be considered a credit to you. It is no good to think it will, or even that it should be. It is for me to prepare you for life, as you will find it. It is my duty to you, and will continue to be."

"I hope it will," murmured Naomi. "Suppose he

changed, and we had to be grateful! It is better to face our accepted goal. It is anyhow familiar."

"We must say goodbye," said Fanny. "The day has been a great one. We shall always remember it."

"And we shall renew it," said her sister. "It will come again. I feel it. It is not the last."

"So it is over," said Hamish to his cousins. "I fear you cannot regret it. I wish it could have been different. I wish my home was more like yours. I suppose you would say the same to me. We all have our reasons."

"I hope Father will drop down dead on his way home," said Ralph. "I really do hope it. I don't know how I am to meet him. And we could repair to the workhouse. It has come to seem homelike."

"Do you suppose we have to work there?" said Naomi. "Does Father know the meaning of the word? What does he think we can do? He would hardly feel we could be useful. And the people there dislike work. That is how they come to enter. Perhaps the name holds a challenge."

"What is the subject?" said Simon, overtaking them. "Do not tell me it is the only one."

"You have said it, sir," said Graham.

"I suppose your life is narrow," said Simon, in another tone. "There is the lack of interest, the limited outlook. But the paucity of your ideas, your poverty of thought! It troubles me. I do not know what to say."

"Then let him avoid the topic," muttered Ralph. "It is his standby as much as ours. Who else started it?"

"I am not going to bind myself to silence on the subject, to swear that the word shall not pass my lips. If you copy me, it is not my fault. You say it is my main subject. What other have you? You had better let me hear it."

"Here is Hamish coming back with us," said Julia, overtaking them with Fanny and her nephew. "To make a happy ending to our happy day."

"Happy day," said Emma, who was sitting with her nurse outside the house.

"Is that what you have had?" said Fanny.

Emma made no reply.

"They have had a very nice day, ma'am," said the nurse.

"Why?" said Claud.

"Well, you have been to see your great-uncle on his birthday."

"Not birthday," said Claud.

"Well, perhaps he did not have any presents," said Julia.

"Oh, yes," said Claud, in a shocked tone.

"Well, he did not show them to us."

"Not for us," said Claud, in admonition.

"All for Uncle Edwin!" said Emma.

"You understand everything, don't you?" said Fanny.

"Clever girl!" said Emma, doing so once again.

# CHAPTER IX

"It is dishonest to listen at a door," said Claud.

"Yes," said Emma, continuing to do so.

"Miss Dolton says no good person does it."

"She says it about everything. It can't always be true."

"Who is talking in the schoolroom?"

"Hamish and Naomi. They are going to marry each other. Hamish will give Naomi his house, when Uncle Edwin dies. And he is glad she hasn't anything to give to him. Then that made endearment that hadn't any meaning. I knew they had that with each other."

"I don't want Naomi to live with Hamish."

"Neither do I. She is better than Miss Dolton. It is always the best who have to go. Of course they generally die."

"She is too old to marry."

"Not much. She is twenty-one. You can marry when you are older."

"Then she is too young. She is not like a married person. And Hamish has Aunt Rhoda and Uncle Edwin. Naomi is not his."

"Everyone belongs to someone before she marries."

"Father will forbid her to do it."

"I don't think he can. Marrying is different. And Hamish would not obey."

"I don't want it to happen," said Claud, with tears in his voice.

"Neither do I. Why should Hamish take what is ours?"

"Whatever is wrong?" said Simon, from the landing below.

"Naomi belongs to us," said Claud. "We don't want Hamish to marry her. Her home is here."

There was a pause.

"Oh, he will not do that. It is not a thing that could happen. They are too nearly related to marry."

"You will forbid it?" said Emma, her tone rising. "But you don't know how much they will mind."

"What makes you think they want to marry?"

"I heard them through the door."

"You must not listen at doors. It is a thing we never do."

"She doesn't often," said Claud. "You might almost say never."

"We must say it quite. And you must not speak of what you heard. That is as wrong as listening. You must just forget it."

"I can't do that," said Emma. "I remember everything."

"She can't help it," said Claud. "Her memory is above the average."

"Well, put it out of your minds, and run away and be happy."

"How can anyone do that?" said Claud.

"You have everything to make you so. A pleasant home and every care and comfort."

"You could have all that in the workhouse," said Emma. "I suppose you would, when you were young."

"And when you were ill," said her brother.

"You need not think about the workhouse. It is nothing to do with you."

"It is in our old age, that it will be our refuge," said Emma, in an informative manner. "And that creeps on us all."

"So it will not happen," said Claud, as his father left them. "I somehow knew it couldn't. But it is not true that relations can't marry. The gardener married his cousin. You and I will have to wait, until we are too old for Father to forbid it."

"Or until he is too old to understand," said Simon's daughter.

Simon looked quickly at Hamish and Naomi, as they

entered the library. The group from the other house had been bidden to luncheon, and the elders had just arrived.

"So you came on before your parents, Hamish. You might have let us have your company. How long have you been in the house?"

"Most of the morning, sir. I have been with Naomi. To me the time seemed short."

"I missed you in my study. I was to explain something to you."

"You must forgive me, sir. You will, when you hear my reason. This is a great day to me. It is the day of my life. I think you understnad me. I hope you have nothing against me as a son-in-law?"

"But of course I have," said Simon, lightly. "You and Naomi are cousins twice over, doubly bound by blood. You might as well marry your sister."

"I have often wished she was that. But she was not, and I have lived to be glad of it. There is nothing against our marriage. I am sure you will give your consent."

"You can hardly be saying what you mean. Of course I cannot give it. You must see how unwise it would be, see the folly and the risk. You have wished Naomi was your sister. You have almost had your wish. You can have it now. But it must be enough."

"You know it cannot be, sir. Your own life must have taught you. As a man yourself, you understand. And as Naomi's father, you cannot be surprised."

"It is not a thing to be thought of. The tie of blood puts it out of court. I regret that you have been thrown together. But the relationship made it inevitable. And you would naturally have taken it as precluding anything further. I deeply deplore such marriages. I could never give my sanction."

"Mother, what do you feel?" said Hamish.

"What your cousin does. My son, I have to say it. If only I could think with both of you! How I wish it!"

"What do you feel, Aunt Fanny?"

"What my husband does. I see it would be unwise. But my feeling is hardly so strong."

"What is yours, Aunt Julia?"

"Those words will do for me. I have no better ones."

"Father, what do you feel?" said Hamish, with hope in his tone.

"I must agree with Naomi's father. He feels what I should feel in his place. I feel it in my own. Like your mother I have to say it."

"What do Naomi's brothers think?"

"If I am to lose my sister," said Graham, "I would rather lose her to someone near and known to me. I do not understand the risk. I did not know it was so great."

"I will copy my grandmother, and say I have no better words," said Ralph.

"What does my Naomi feel?" said Fanny.

"What Hamish does. I hardly need to say it."

"Ah, no, my dear," said Simon. "You will listen to your father. You are the nearest to him of his children. You will spare him this anxiety and grief."

"No one has asked me what I feel," said Walter. "So I am not as sorry as I might be, to say I support my brother."

"Ah, Walter, how often you have done so!" said Simon.

"You surprise me, Cousin Walter," said Hamish. "And so does my father. I should have thought you would think for yourselves. I did not know that everyone's words would do for everyone else."

"They may be the only possible ones," said Simon.

"You realise that mine were different?" said Graham.

"And I said they could be mine," said Ralph. "I have a subtle courage."

"Well, I suppose we may have some luncheon," said Simon.

"Ought we to eat?" said Ralph. "Until this matter is behind?"

"Our guests should do so," said Simon, striding to the door. "And the matter is as you put it."

"How are we to sit?" said Hamish.

"As you always do," said Simon. "Yes, you may sit by Naomi. You have been brought up as brother and sister, and can feel it is what you are. I have never prevented your friendship."

"I wonder he has not," said Graham to Ralph, "as he feels what he does."

"And I wonder at my father," said Hamish. "People's actions as well as their words seem the same for them all."

"Is there so much against the marriage of cousins?" said Ralph. "The Greeks allowed children of the same father to marry."

"We are not the Greeks," said Simon, flushing. "And we might be no better, if we were. In that way we should not be."

"No one can prove he is what he is supposed to be. Every kind of marriage must take place."

"Few of us need any proof, as you know quite well."

"So we have reached a deadlock," said Ralph.

"For the moment," said Hamish. "But time will pass, and other things with it. People will accept what has to be. We shall not waver or change."

"Time will work in you as well as in them," said Simon. "You are right to let it have its way. We find it takes it."

"We do. And we are ready to trust it. It is the same as trusting each other."

"You feel that at the moment," said Sir Edwin. "You would be ashamed not to feel it. But nature has its way as well as time. We can leave them to work together."

"You seem to think they can only work in one direction, Father."

"They tend to the one. Things grow and fade; they are born and die. Everything goes the same way."

"Shall we remember that there are other subjects?" said Simon.

"We hardly can," said Graham. "There is only this, while it is with us."

"Perhaps we are doing them no kindness. Our touch on it can hardly be welcome. And I am not talking of mine more than of yours."

"I think you might be, sir. And so will they."

"Surely other views can be taken," said Ralph. "The matter does not go without saying like this."

"It has not done so," said Simon. "But perhaps it may go without any more saying."

"Go in what way?" said Hamish.

"We must leave the matter," said Sir Edwin. "For us it has come to an end."

"Mother, would you not like to have Naomi for a daughter?"

"My Naomi! How I should like it! But I have known her as my sister's. I have liked that too much to end it. Do not take it from me."

"What is there behind it all? There seems to be a sort of conspiracy. Did you foresee the question, and agree on a common line?"

"We did not," said Simon. "It was not a thing to be foreseen."

"There is something I do not understand."

"Ah, how seldom we do that!" said Rhoda. "We cannot lighten the dark. It is too hard a thing."

"We must talk to our parents by themselves," said Naomi. "We cannot do much in a general discussion."

"Ah, do not, my dear," said Simon. "Do something for your father. Leave the matter where it is. It is the first thing he has asked of you. You trust each other, and you trust time. Follow your own belief."

"In itself it would be a good thing, sir," said Ralph. "It would keep Naomi with us. And you would see your descendants where you once hoped to see them."

"Do you think I have not thought of it? And that it would count to me, compared with my conscience? Do you think I am a father or not?"

"I have not always seen signs of it."

"It seems you do not now. Perhaps you do not recognise them. They may not be on the surface."

"No, it is true that they may not."

"You appear to think you are the subject of discussion."

"I am about to be," said Graham. "My future is secure. I have been offered a post at Oxford. A college is better than the alternative, though I should think they have something in common. All institutions have the same soul."

"I am glad indeed," said Simon. "I hope Ralph will do as well."

"They came up and outshone me," said Hamish. "My place was clear. It was a good thing I had not to earn my bread, as I was the least able to."

"It is one I should find little fault with," said Ralph.

"I found a good deal. But I find it no longer. I can offer a home to Naomi, without asking her to wait for it. She will bear with my being a subordinate inmate of it."

"You must remember it yourself," said Sir Edwin, speaking with an effort. "I dislike to remind you of it, but you are offering a home that is not yours. While it is mine, you will not do so. You have heard what we have said."

"Father, I can hardly believe my ears, or accept the words as yours. They seem so unnatural in you. I wonder if I hear them."

"I am glad you find them strange on my lips. That is all I can say."

"You might as well say you will disinherit me, if I live the life that is my own."

"I thought perhaps I should say it. I could not utter the words."

"Perhaps we could wait for a while," said Julia, "and see if they continue in this mind. And in that case regard the objections as outweighed by their feeling."

"That is what I was going to say," said Fanny.

"I am glad you did not say it," said Simon. "You are my wife, and have heard what I said. Surely that is enough."

"I must have a mind of my own. I am not an echo of you. It is not what you have asked of me."

"You should support me in a difficult place. You have many times done so. Fanny, will you not do so now?"

"It is a hard place for many of us. And there does not seem enough reason. I cannot feel there is."

"Fanny, you must trust me. I have knowledge of these matters that you have not."

"I do not know how you have got it. You have not thought of them. You are not a stranger to me."

"My wife, do not be one to me."

"Several of us are strangers to each other," said Naomi. "I begin to wonder what anyone is."

"Try to be what you are, my dear," said Simon. "What you are to your father."

"I look forward to discussing it up in the school-room," said Ralph. "I am not at ease on this floor. Early memories are too much."

"I will come up with you, if I may," said Hamish.

"Yes, go and be together," said Simon, in a full tone. "Go and be what you have always been. You will find it is enough."

"Father is seeing us as worthy of trust," said Graham, as they went, "or anyhow showing that he does so."

"So my home is no good to me," said Hamish. "The workhouse might have been better, and may be so. At any rate Naomi and I could be together."

"They separate the men and women there," said Ralph.

"Well, then it would be no worse. This is a senseless struggle. We cannot break up our lives without a ground. We must take things into our own hands. I would not choose to do it. It is my nature to go where I am led. But I am a man like any other, when I am placed like this."

"I wish I had a chance to describe myself as fully," said Walter, who had followed them.

"You need not envy me the occasion."

"I envy what arises from it, the place in the limelight,

the chance to appear in your true colours. I do feel it a pity that mine are hidden. And your opportunity to submit to fate with dignity and disregard of self. You would not let it escape you? It is a chance to show greatness."

"Greatness may not be achieved only at one's own expense. I think it usually is not."

"I should so like to show it. It must be in me, as it is in everyone, though I don't know who found that out. It is the chance to prove it that is rare."

"It must be," said Naomi. "We seldom see it. I think I never have."

"We are to see it now," said Walter. "I envy you all, and you and Hamish the most. You will leave an impression on us, that will last our lives."

"It is no good, Uncle," said Naomi. "The cost of giving it would last ours. You must go back and tell Father you have failed. You can tell him, if you like, that it is a great failure."

"It will be denied its greatness," said Graham. "And a great failure tends to have some success in it."

"There will be none in this," said Naomi. "Uncle knows we shall not yield. He would not in our place. He could not have proved it better. Father makes it hard for us, especially for me, but we must simply turn our eyes from it. There is nothing against our marriage. We are not people apart. If there are reasons in anyone's mind, they should not be there. That is all that can be said."

"Yes," said Walter, slowly, "I see it is. All that can be said by you at the moment, in your place. I will go to your father and tell him I have failed. It is not a great failure, and he will not think it is."

"Whatever is behind it?" said Hamish. "There is something that is not said. Is your father jealous, Naomi? He would lose you less to me than to anyone else."

"No, not unless he hides it. He has never had those feelings. He is not an emotional father. You know what he has been."

"He is a stranger to me. I did not know it, but he is. And my father is even more so. And naturally I did not know that."

"I must say it again," said Ralph. "It would be an auspicious marriage. Naomi would live in the family shelter instead of the public one. And Father's fears would be at rest. He should be the first to see it."

"Has he become too fond of his picture to give it up?" said Naomi. "He has never given any sign of affection for it."

"He never foretold such things for you, as he did for us," said Graham. "He would like you to carry on his line where he thought it would be. Though it would be through a daughter, the blood would be the same. Hamish must be right that there is something else."

"I dislike these mysterious days," said Ralph. "Is our childhood to be the happiest time of our life? I almost wish it would return."

"So do I," said his mother, opening the door. "They were simple days, if they were dull and bleak ones. And I was happy in them, or enough to think so now. There was none of this mystery and strong feeling unexplained. It is strange to be perplexed by the people you have lived with for half your life. Your grandmother and I seem to stand by ourselves, and to be at a loss for the reason."

"Have you come to give us your sympathy?" said Naomi. "We welcome nothing else."

"Yes, I have, my child, and to ask for yours. I am in great and simple need of it. There is a feeling between your father and me, that there has never been. We have differed and held our own, but we have never been apart. There has never been this strange, new distance. I cannot see this question of your marriage as he does. The obstacle does not seem to me so great. To tell you the truth, I have thought it might happen. To tell you more, I have hoped it would. To tell the whole, I should like it to do so now. It may be to say that I am a woman and a mother, but what is there

123

against my being both? And what is there to prevent it? And why should I be any better, if I were neither?"

"Power is vested in such things," said Hamish. "If it is to be used for us, our way is clear. But I wish it had not happened as it has. It seemed an almost sinister thing. I hope we shall not remember it. But we know we shall."

"Then is Father to be set at nought?" said Ralph. "I did not know it could be."

"It cannot," said Simon, from the doorway. "It will not, and I must face the result, the hostility of my family, the trouble for myself. I must meet it as a personal sorrow and suffer it as such. I cannot alter what I have said. I wish I could. If you knew how much I wish it! I have not wished even for the one thing more. But I must follow my conscience, if I do so alone."

There was a silence before Hamish answered in a quiet tone.

"I must say the same to you, sir. We should understand each other, if we understand nothing else. And more I do not understand. I too must suffer the trouble for myself, the greater that Naomi must share it. It will do no good to say more."

"I must say one word. I must trust you to do nothing at the time. To remember your youth and ignorance, and what is due to those to whom your debt is great. And due also to Naomi, due to yourself."

"I promise it, sir. It is a thing you have a right to ask. I am troubled by our difference, wish I could see it in its true light. But I must say I know I do not do so, and that in the end I must claim the right of every man to judge his cause for himself."

Simon went down to the library and summoned his brother.

"Walter, we are living the evil days. I wish I had been happier, while they came not. I wish I had ensured that they should not come. I should have left the place, and put the helpless people out of harm. But my heart was here, and my roots were deep. I could not do it, and the harm is done. I wish I could leave it, shut my eyes to the danger and the wrong. But my daughter! Can I fail her in this crisis of her life? Can I do anything but the thing I feel I cannot do? Anything but tell the truth?"

"Simon, I wish you could. We know the risk is small. And the trouble you would cause, is great. If we weigh one against the other, on which side does the balance fall? Which would Naomi choose, if she were outside the truth? You have been so much the master of them all, the mentor, the absolute head. It would all be seen as empty, as a pose. Can you face it, and go on after it? If you know you cannot, is it any good to try?"

"I can do what I must, as we all can. And face the result, as we face what we cannot escape. And we must take account of my uncle. He would countenance no breach of faith. He would see the question in one way and no other, would not weigh the sides. We saw and heard him, when it arose."

"Simon, I see and hear you and your family."

"They will see the truth as it is. They will see I have expiated the early wrong, continue to expiate it. Yes, it is a sorry place for their head."

"You are the hero of a tragedy. It is a pity you are the villain as well. I am humbled before your complex part."

"I know you dread it with me, for me, for yourself. My dread is for Hamish and Naomi, for the ending of their hope. I pity myself for my sight of it. My own exposure should seem a secondary thing. I must see it as it is."

"It is a hard pass, Simon. I wish we were on the further side. What is to be done? How is the disclosure to be made?"

"I must simply make it. There is no cover and no escape. I must ask Rhoda for her wishes and try to follow them. Wishes! It is an ironic word. If only I could spare her! We had better get this first step over. Are she and my uncle in the house?"

"They are alone in the morning-room. Fanny is still upstairs. And Mater is somewhere by herself. The time is as good as any other."

"There is no good time. You will come with me, Walter? It will be better for me, if you are there."

"I will come indeed. We must be able to discuss it. And I would not miss any stage in the drama. I am so absorbed in it."

"I shall depend on your help," said Simon, realising that he was being given it. "We will face the moment. It is nothing by the one that is to come."

Sir Edwin and Rhoda were standing silent, having come to the end of their words. They turned, as the brothers came to them, and Simon spoke.

"Uncle, Hamish and Naomi will marry in spite of us, will take the matter into their own hands. What is to be done?"

"The one thing. I saw they were unshaken. And I see, as you do, the one course."

"I do not feel with you," said Rhoda. "To me it is a wrong one. It would turn risk into a certainty. It would break up innocent lives. It would bring shame on you and me and Simon. On you, Edwin; for you would be seen to have no son, to have lived a lie. It serves an old man's conscience at the expense of youth. At the cost of the family name; for nothing that is told, can be hidden. Should we sacrifice so much to gain so little?"

"It is the thing that must be gained."

"I see it must," said Simon.

"I cannot see it. Are you not in love with sacrifice? Your clear conscience, your clean breast, will they not cost too dear? Cost others too dear, I mean; they may serve yourself. And have you thought what the moment would be! Think while there is time."

"I have thought," said Simon.

"How will you break the truth? Will you contrive a scene, put on an act? Call your family together, to undo

126

yourself in their eyes? In the prime of your life and your fatherhood?"

"It is what I shall do. It is not an act."

"I would rather die than have Hamish know."

"I feel the same. I dare not tell my children. But I shall do so. And we know we shall not die."

"My life is at an end," said Sir Edwin. "My time of durance will be short. I can the better judge of yours."

"You are both too self-righteous," said Rhoda. "You should see yourselves as they would see you. And I will not consent to the confession. I have the right to decide. Such a thing is settled by the woman. You are anxious to do no wrong to anyone. Then see that you do none."

"I must face the wrong I have done," said Simon.

"I will not be there when you speak. I will not face the pain for others and myself. I meant what I said. It is needless and not only mine."

"You had better be there," said Walter. "The numbers will protect you. The meeting with Hamish afterwards will be saved from the worst. Everyone should be there, as it will ease things for all."

"It is too great a retribution," said Simon. "I see it with Rhoda's eyes."

"It is," said Sir Edwin. "Civilised life exacts its toll. We live among the civilised."

"The conventions are on the surface," said his wife. "We know the natural life is underneath."

"We do; we have our reason. But we cannot live it. We know the consequences of doing so. If not, we learn."

"I shall never think quite the same of you, Edwin."

"The moment comes to most of us with each other. It came to me with you. I am happy in the time of my downfall. It is late."

"I am not," said Simon. "It could not be better chosen by a hostile fate."

"Would you like me to say the word?" said Walter. "It would be better for me, as I am not involved."

"No, I must say it myself. I could not stand by and hear it said, afraid to do my own penance, humbler than I had reason to be. I shall fall in the eyes of my wife, see my effort for my sons wasted, take from my daughter the meaning of her youth. And this to avoid something that in some days would have been lawful and right!"

"We live in our own," said Sir Edwin.

"What Simon and I did, is done in all days," said Rhoda.

# CHAPTER X

"Hamish thinks you should be going," said Fanny, coming into the room with her nephew and her children. "Simon and Walter have had the most of you, and it seems soon to say good-bye. Here is their mother come to say it with us."

"I wondered if it would ever be said," said Graham. "When have hours held so much?"

"They are to hold more," said Walter, in a low tone. "You must be ready for it."

"It cannot be said yet," said Simon, standing still and seeming to hold his voice from defining his words. "I must keep you for a while. There is something else to be said. It is I who must say it. It will take only a moment. It is what will follow, that may be long. I dread it. I have reason to. I have thought of it for twenty-four years. I see now that I have. I trusted the time might never come. But it is here, and we must face it. It is I who have brought it on us. It is I who face the most."

"Then say it, my son," said Julia. "Do not ask more of yourself and us. A word is soon said, and waiting for it must be what it is. We shall imagine more than the truth, and the picture may never quite fade. Let us face it and forget it. That is best."

"If it can be so," said Simon. "But it cannot be. It is because it cannot be forgotten, that it must be said. It throws its light on much that has been dark, on much that has been so to-day. You have felt the need of light.— Hamish is my son. He is Rhoda's child and mine. We were together in my uncle's house after their marriage. They did not live as man and wife. My uncle accepted the child as his. He was its legal father. He has been one in every sense.

He will remain so. Hamish will be his heir. But we must know the truth that lies beneath. There can be no marriage between Hamish and my daughter. They are half-brother and sister as well as sisters' children. The dangers would be too great."

There was a pause.

"I thought my father was different," said Hamish, as if the words broke out. "Not as other fathers were. I see it now. I see it all. But he will be my father."

"I shall," said Sir Edwin. "You will be my son. You have been so in spite of the difference. There has been no difference in you. We shall not change to each other. That is, you will not to me. For me of course there is no change."

"Mother, you are my mother!" said Hamish.

"My son, how much more that I have harmed you! That I have taken from you something that was yours! That I have made for you the difference you have seen! I am doubly so."

"Naomi, I am your father," said Simon. "And more so for what you know."

Naomi did not speak.

"We shall be the closer for the threat to us," said Hamish, moving to her. "And it is no more than a threat. There is no need to act on a truth that might never have emerged. It would not have in most cases, should not have to my mind. Many must lie unsaid. We can put it from us and go forward."

There was a pause, as the denial of this seemed stronger, that it was silent.

"Simon, there has been this between us," said Fanny. "This in your mind through all our years. The truth is taken from our marriage, more than if you had told it. You lost your inheritance. Now you have lost your wife. How much you have lost!"

"My dear, I should not have had you for a wife. Or I might not, and you know it. Your own words prove it, show the risk we should have run. And it was better that we should marry, for you as well as for me."

"My sister!" said Rhoda. "How I have longed to tell you, needed your sympathy and your reproach! How much better I should have been for both! But it might have done harm to so many, prevented so much. It might have prevented much for you."

"It might have been right to prevent it. The truth should have been allowed to take its course. But there are my five children. What is there for me to say?"

"That you are glad it did not take it," said Simon, "glad you did not know. There is nothing else to be said."

"My son," said Julia, "I am always your mother. I am not less so for what I have heard. But I must say to-day what I never thought to say. I am glad your father is not with us."

"If he were, nothing would have happened, nothing of good or ill. My uncle would not have married. Hamish would not exist. Fanny might not have wanted to leave her sister. It has all followed from his death. And we can hardly wish it all undone. And of course you are less my mother, when that is what you say to me, at this moment in your life and mine. I hope I may not be less your son."

"I suppose you knew, Walter?" said Julia. "You have always known?"

"I knew before Hamish was born, before Uncle Edwin knew. You see it was my right."

"When Uncle Edwin knew!" said Ralph, before he thought. "That must have been a moment."

"It was not what you think," said Walter.

"It was not," said Simon. "And you can surely think again. Your great-uncle is what you know."

"Ah, how I have found it!" said Rhoda. "How I find it still! How I look always to find it!"

"What have you to say to me, Graham?" said Simon.

"What one man must say to another, sir. I understand it, regret it, feel for you that it has had to be revealed. That is a piece of ill fortune many would escape."

"I did not look for talk from man to man," said Simon, after a pause. "Speak to me as a son to his father. That is what I meant."

"Then I feel that your words have meant little, sir. And always less than they should have. I can hardly feel anything else, or expect to be believed, if I said it."

"What have you to say to me, Ralph? Speak without temper, so that I can judge of it."

"Very much what Graham has said, sir. It is the only thing we can say. I have thought you hard and self-righteous; and I now feel you were both, and should have been neither."

"Hard and self-righteous! So that is what you feel we should not be," said Simon, looking at his sons.

"This was only one stumble," said Graham. "We must not judge it as more than it is."

"Again as man to man," said his father.

"Simon, if you ask for opinions, you will hear them," said Fanny. "And what did you look to hear?"

"My Naomi, what do you feel?" said Simon.

"I think this should be forgotten, that it should not have been revealed. Men keep their early troubles to themselves. They behave as if they had not been. And in some times and places children of one father have married."

"My dear, do not make it worse for me. It is bad enough. If you knew how I tried to take that view, how hardly I gave it up! It is for you, not for myself, that I have told the truth. For myself should I have done so? For myself I kept silence for twenty-four years. Thought of you has forced me to break it. And it was only one stumble, as my kind son has said."

"I think he was kind, Father. I think you are not to them, that you often have not been."

"Then be kind to me now. You judge the want of kindness. And it is true that I have been embittered by the turn of my life, and betrayed it in dealing with theirs. Show me kindness now in my need of it."

"Why were you so embittered? Hamish was your son. And everything would have gone to a son in the end."

"I will tell the truth. I wanted for myself what was always to have been mine. The thought was the foundation of my boyhood. And I had looked to leave it to an acknowledged son. You think it all looms too large to me. I know it does. I do not deny or explain it. I accept it even from myself. I must be what I am."

"I do not want the inheritance," said Hamish. "I have not cared for the place in that measure. Your feeling for it makes it yours. And I have no real right to it. Yours is the first claim. When my father dies—you know whom I mean by my father—he will leave it to you, and make me a small provision. My needs will be slight. I shall never marry, as I cannot marry Naomi. I could not accept anyone else in her stead. I could never think of her as my sister. It is no help to me to feel she is that. It startles me that anyone should think so. That is my last word, the only one I have to say."

"I have my word, Hamish," said Sir Edwin. "It is my only one, as yours is. I shall leave the place to you, as what you are in name, and must not cease to be. If it is a millstone about your neck, you will carry it. You will fulfil your part in life, knowing it is yours. What we know further is not for us to pursue. It is not our own knowledge. We must not use it as such."

"I see you are right, Uncle," said Simon. "Nothing else would fill the need. The truth must lie underneath, as it has lain. How I wish it need not have been thrown into the light! How I tried to see another way! But we could not see one. There was none."

"I will go away," said Hamish. "I must go to other places, and must go far. I am going for Naomi's sake and mine. We cannot meet in our new character, until we have suppressed the old, learned to pretend it has not been. I shall never be resigned to the truth, never find it natural, never do more than act a part. But that I must do before I return. And that she must learn to do by herself. It would not help us to be together. It would indeed be of little good. It is a thing each must do alone."

"You may go, my son," said Sir Edwin, using the words for the first time in his life. "But return in time for us to part. This does not serve as our farewell. And as your road lengthens, mine grows short."

"I must say the same," said Rhoda. "You may go, my son. But return in the end to your mother."

Simon turned to his daughter, knowing that for her there was no help; and she understood him and let him draw her to his side.

"I wish Shakespeare was here," said Walter, to break the tension. "I mean, I wish I was he. If I was, I could make so much of the scene. It is sad that it has to be wasted."

"Can you bring it to an end?" said Simon. "He would have done so. And it is not the easiest part."

"I am jealous of you, Simon. I did not know you were so like him."

"I will do it," said Sir Edwin. "It is time for us to leave you. My method is not Shakespeare's, but it will serve. And his is not always so different. We will not offer our thanks; that can hardly be; but we have some cause to be grateful."

Hamish looked after his parents, and did not follow them. Sir Edwin glanced at him and said nothing, and he turned to Simon.

"Cousin Simon—as you will be to me—I have a last word to say. I cannot dispute my father's decision. He is too old to contend with, to turn from his mind. But after his death I will make the change. I will transfer everything to you, and keep only a competence. You are the next in the line, where I have no place. I was born before your marriage. The empty legal right I do not count. And I do not want the position or the duty it carries. You know why I was glad to have it. I have not that reason now. Graham will be your heir, as he should be. And other things will be as they should have been. That is all I have to say."

"Have a care," said Simon. "Take thought for your words. That is how you feel now. It is natural that your mind should be disturbed. But the hour will pass, and the mood with it. You will want what is yours, as all men want it. You will have your use for it, as all men have. You are not as unusual as you think; none of us is. Forget what you have said, as I will forget it. Remember the claims that lie ahead. Go on your journey. Return to your father for his last days. That is the duty to your hand. And leave the future, as we all leave it."

"Cousin Simon, are you yourself so unusual? Cannot your mood pass, as you say mine can?"

"Be careful, lest it do so. I might remember your words. You might come to wish them unsaid."

"They came from my heart. You may look to the time you will not accept. I shall unsay nothing."

"You will unsay what you will. I will wait for you to do so. I will welcome you with the retraction on your lips. It is what I look for, hope for, believe will be. I only ask you to remember it."

Hamish turned to Naomi.

"It is over for us, Naomi. There is nothing left. We may not even ask to be alone. What we have is not of any help, and can never be. It is the thing that takes away our life. But there will always be our feeling under those that may be shown. When we are young and old, it will be in us, always there. We must try to feel it is not nothing, and ask no more."

"A thing is not nothing, when it is all there is. It is like those that help prisoners to keep their reason. We shall feel what people do not know, what those who do know will forget. We shall have something of what we were to have, the shadow of it, kept underneath. And we shall always have it."

Hamish turned and left the room. Simon a moment later did the same, signing to his wife to follow. And Walter and his niece and nephews were alone.

"So you wish you were Shakespeare, Uncle," said Graham at once. "We must all wish we were something else. We are no longer what we were. We see Father cast from his height, and resent his overthrow as much as his occupation of it. Our life has no meaning, in so far as he dominated it. And as that was fully, we look back on nothing."

"What a mountain of consequence to follow from what was not much more!" said Ralph. "And the disproportion does no good."

"Naomi is above us all," said Graham, saying what had to be said. "She knows the depths, and that sets people high. We look up from our lower place."

"We do. We shall always know how low it is. She has taught us what Father has not."

"Father had to show great courage," said Graham. "It was terrible to see him showing it. We had only seen him making a demand on it before. I minded it much more, than if I had never cringed before him."

"I minded it less," said Ralph.

"I minded the waste of my years of silence," said Walter. "I had kept the secret, and felt how safe it was with me. And it had been in danger. I was no real protector of it."

"Imagine the moment when the truth was broken to Uncle Edwin!" said Ralph. "If you dare to think of it."

"We hardly seemed to know of one. The child was accepted as his. He himself accepted it. Nothing was said at the time. I do not know what passed between him and your father."

"It is a sinister sign," said Naomi, speaking for the first time. "That even you do not know."

"I am not ashamed of it. Human lips could not frame the words. And clearly your father's could not."

"Will Hamish really give up the place to Father?" said Ralph. "What a waste of our clouded youth!"

"It may not be in your case," said Naomi. "Graham is the eldest son. You may continue on the old line."

"We have never asked you to explain your feeling for Father, Uncle."

"No, you have not. And I do not feel you should have."

"How did you feel, when you heard what was to happen, that there was to be a child? It is a time I cannot imagine."

"I am not going to help you. You see, I do not have to imagine it."

"You dare not recall it," said Graham. "And there is no need. It is graven on your heart."

"So Hamish is our half-brother," said Ralph. "We have been absorbed in his being Naomi's. He did not say what he felt about gaining two brothers."

"Did you expect him to say that after all some good had come out of it?" said Naomi.

"I wonder what he feels about his mother's part in the matter."

"It is a thing I dared not say," said Graham.

"I have not dared to think of it," said Walter. "And I will not now."

"I find I must," said Ralph. "My thoughts return to it. It is the strangest point in the story."

"I cannot think how you can deal in such thoughts and words," said Naomi.

"There is a vein of something in him, that is not in us," said Graham.

"I am only more open," said his brother.

"A dubious quality," said Naomi. "When people are being that, it is best to lower your opinion of them at once. Before they have time to lower it of other people or of you. And to do it enough to be indifferent to what they say."

"To continue to be so," said Ralph, "I should like to hear what is passing between our parents."

"You have lowered our opinion of you," said Graham.

"I wonder how our great-uncle feels about it all. About having no son, when he has been seen as having one. And about the disclosure concerning his wife."

"What everyone would feel," said Graham. "Simple and

deep unease. It is Father who has the extreme part. He has always been seen as a law to himself. Well, we must accept that it is what he was."

"What does Hamish feel about being Father's son? A thing I thought no one could suffer but ourselves."

"As you are versed in the matter," said Naomi, "you do not need instruction on it."

"I have been one all my life. But what is it to become one suddenly? Well, he has escaped twenty-four years of it."

"He has escaped being Uncle Edwin's son as well. He has missed it all."

"It seems that our life must be different, now that we know the truth. And now that Father may soon inherit everything."

"Your life will be the same," said Simon's voice. "Yes, I heard what you said. It was my duty to do so. You will not build on what may not happen, on what I hope will never be. We do not accept a word uttered in an hour of shock. It is with me as if I had not heard. It must be so with you."

"Hamish meant it, Father," said Naomi. "You can take his word as it was said. He has never valued his place for himself. He was only glad to give so much to me. It is best to see the future as it is. You can look forward and see yourself the head of the house and the family."

"And my Naomi the daughter of them both," said Simon, putting his arm about her. "We will make up a fairy tale together. We will be the king and the princess in it. But we will remember that is what it is."

"It is more than that," said Graham, as his father and sister moved aside. "It would be Father's dream realised, the hope of his youth restored. It would raise him to his level, make him the man he should have been. We ought to want to see it. But we hardly know if we do."

"We pity the results of his lapse," said Ralph. "But should he be actually compensated for them?"

"He has not been," said Walter. "He has lived the years

138

you have seen. Whatever his future may be, they will lie behind. One view might be that he has suffered enough."

"I can't help half-liking him to suffer. He has always half-liked me to; I believe even quite liked it."

"He was anxious abour our uncertain future," said Graham, "and felt he should prepare us for it."

"It is too soon for you to be mellowed by prosperity. We are still to look to our settled fate."

"And you still harp on it," said Simon, returning to the group. "I need have no fears about your ideas of the future. The old ones seem to be enough. My lesson has gone deep. I can congratulate myself on it."

"But not on everything else," muttered his son.

Simon came to dinner in an absent manner, conscious of his altered character in the eyes of his family. He saw his words in the light of their knowledge, and hesitating to speak in his usual manner, spoke little.

"What a long day this has seemed!" said his mother, meaning to break a silence.

"It has brought us a different father," murmured Ralph. "And we can see he knows it."

"It has brought me another son," said Simon, turning to him. "I think you are more exposed than I am. You have not dared to show your real self before. I wonder you do so now. I am not the only person present. Your mother and sister see you as you are."

"Then you and I are on equal ground, sir."

"We are all exposed," said Walter. "The day has been a test. And if we have all withstood it but one, it is a good average."

"I have seen it and thought so," said Simon. "It has been a help to me. Only one of us, as you say, has failed."

"Will Hamish really transfer the place to you, Simon, after his father's—your uncle's death?" said Julia.

"He will," said Naomi. "I know his mind. He will not live in that house without me. He has seen it from a boy as his home and mine."

"From a boy!" said Simon. "What harm has been done!"

"So Father's confession may have restored him to it," said Ralph. "It would be an ironic fate."

"After twenty-four years," said Walter. "It is what it would be."

"It is Naomi who has lost it. She must see things in her own light."

"Which of us needs to be told that?" said Simon. "She or I?"

"Or her mother?" said Fanny.

"In your place I should wish I had not told the truth, sir," said Ralph.

"I wish I had had any choice but to tell it."

"I should wish it for Naomi's sake."

"It was for her sake that I told it, as you know. Why do you think you have this score to pay off? I have done my duty to you."

"As you saw it," said his son.

"Duty is seldom liked either by the doer or the object," said Fanny. "And why should it be? It is not often of advantage to either."

"So we are to forget Hamish's promise, sir?" said Graham. "I am to take the post at Oxford, anyhow for the time?"

"Yes, and probably for always. We must put the idea from our minds. It is likely it will be forgotten, and I hope it from my heart. If Hamish should hold to it, I should be in his hands. I should succeed to my uncle's place, and you in your turn to mine. You would relinquish other claims, and do your duty here, as you had seen it done. Ralph might say it was not all you had seen. So I have said it for him. It is not hard to supply his words."

"And this is putting it out of your minds!" said Ralph.

"We shall think you are envious of Graham, if you continue in this vein."

"How could I be, when the matter is to be forgotten? You are the person who remembers it."

"There has never been any feeling like that between the brothers," said Julia.

"There has never been this between them before."

"What would Naomi choose, as things are now?" said Ralph.

"I have no choice," said his sister. "It makes no difference."

"It would make a little, my dear," said Simon. "I would see that it did."

"If the prospect is not a likely one, Hamish is the person who knows it," said Ralph.

"He would not wish that said," said Simon. "He was to be taken as knowing his mind. His boyhood is over."

"It is true that it is," said Naomi.

"His wish will be respected," muttered Ralph. "Father said he could supply my words. I can do the same for him."

"Who is that at the door?" said Fanny. "Oh, it is the children."

"Shut the door, Claud," said Simon.

"No, it is Emma's turn."

"Shut it for her, as you should."

"She doesn't want it shut. She leaves doors open. I am shutting it for you."

"We ought to be in bed," said Emma, looking at her grandmother. "But it is a holiday to-morrow, and the Dolt —Miss Dolton doesn't mind if we are late."

"Who is the Dolt?" said Julia, gravely.

"We don't mean she is really a dolt," said Claud. "It is a shortening of her name."

"An abbreviation," said Emma.

"Do you mean it is a pet name?" said Graham.

The children looked at each other, and almost smiled.

"Is it true that we are going to be rich?" said Claud.

"No, it is not," said Simon. "Who told you such a thing?"

"Nurse said something had come through. She didn't know any more."

"It is true that we are poor now," said Emma. "The nursery teapot is cracked."

"Well, perhaps you can have another," said Fanny.

"Oh, it will hold for some time. And it is homely to have it cracked. It is like a book."

"It will make a memory," said Claud.

"It is true that teapots in books are out of repair," said Graham. "I had not thought of it."

"It is the crack that has a meaning," said Emma. "Anyone might have a teapot."

"And have an accident with it," said Ralph.

"That is when the meaning comes. Everyone doesn't have a new one."

"Well, nhoting has happened," said Simon. "There is to be no change."

"Well, we are used to it," said Emma. "And poverty is nothing to be ashamed of."

"I am not ashamed," said Claud. "But perhaps we could have a new book between us."

"One about children," said Emma. "But not meant only for children to read."

"Emma will read it to me. It is a chance that she is more forward. It is no credit to her."

"And none to you either, I suppose?"

Claud fell into mirth.

"Well, you can go to the village with Miss Dolton and choose a book."

"What do you say?" said Julia.

"Thank you, Father," said Emma, turning to the door, and continuing to her brother. "It doesn't seem we are quite so poor. I think something is different. Nurse can feel things, when she doesn't know. I suppose people who don't know much, would have to."

# CHAPTER XI

"Hamish must come, if he is to be in time," said Sir Edwin, as he sat in his library. "I begin to count my days. I shall soon count the hours. I have had many, and except for one time, have not wished them fewer. And I have had the young Hamish, and come to feel him near me. I must see him and say my word before I go. I have not to gather my sheaves. I have none to gather. I have done little, as there was little for me to do. I leave no one the worse for my living, and have not looked for more. I have not seen myself outside my place."

"Hamish will come, Edwin. You need not fear," said Rhoda. "He is on his way."

"It will be hard to be without you, Uncle," said Simon.

"It will scarcely be that. But it will be harder than if you were young. The years have brought us closer. When I lost my brother, I felt you were his son. And that put us on our path."

"I have been glad for my sons to know you, and at an age to be able to do so. It is a thing for them to carry with them."

"A small thing, but perhaps of good. They have seen me as a harmless old man. And it is something to feel in that measure. It does not do nothing."

"I am simply sad," said Fanny. "I cannot say anything else."

"My sister!" said Rhoda. "How I shall need your sadness, its help to me in mine! It is what gives the help."

"The little ones are coming to see you, Uncle. They will come with the boys and Naomi. They will not know——"

"It is goodbye," said Sir Edwin. "It would not matter to them. But it is a thing they may escape."

"How are you, sir?" said Graham, as he led in the group. "We have come upon you in a body. You are good to welcome us."

"I am as you see. And fortunate to be so. At ease after ninety-four years, in every sense."

"We have come to say good-bye," said Claud. "We heard Miss Dolton say so. I don't know why, when you are not going away."

"There is no reason," said Emma, in a low voice. "But when someone is old, it may be a politeness."

"Do you like old people?" said Sir Edwin.

"Yes," said Emma. "We look up to age. I mean when the old person is worthy of it."

"Of course, when people are old, they look as if they are," said Claud.

"Say good-bye to Miss Dolton for me. We have liked each other."

"But she has not been here. How can you say goodbye?"

"It is a mark of respect," whispered Emma. "A good person always respects governesses. I knew about that."

"Would you like a farewell present from me?" said Sir Edwin.

"Yes, please," said Claud. "Of course everyone likes a present. But that is not asking for one."

"Here is half-a-crown for each of you."

"Thank you. That is more than we have ever had. But no one need take care of it for us. We are past that."

"Good-bye," said Sir Edwin, holding out his hand.

"Good-bye. We knew you would say it soon. Of course you can't bear much."

"Kiss your great-uncle's hand," said Julia.

"No," said Claud, drawing back.

"Do as Grandmamma says," said Simon.

"No," said Claud. "We never kiss people's hands."

"You will do as you are told," said Simon.

"No, it is not what you do yourself. You don't set the example."

"That is not the same thing," said Simon, finding himself unprepared to do this. "You must obey me when I speak."

"No, you have told us to do something that is not—" Claud paused for the word.

"Reasonable," said Emma. "Why shouldn't we kiss his face?"

"Well, you may do that," said Fanny.

"Is that any better?" said Sir Edwin.

"Yes," said Claud, as he obeyed. "We don't mind a face being old. It is as good in a way as a young one. Of course there has to be everything."

"I should not have yielded to the elder children," said Simon, as the younger left them.

"But he went too far with them," said Emma's voice. "It is known to have had its result."

"I would never kiss a person's hand," said Claud. "No one is quite so much above us."

"Are my elder great-niece and nephews to spend an hour with me?" said Sir Edwin.

"If they may," said Julia. "Miss Dolton has come for the younger. She is always so reliable and thoughtful."

"I would not stay where I was called such things," said Ralph.

"Then you would not stay anywhere," said Simon. "And possibly will not."

"Well, I can settle in the final refuge, where such qualities are not expected. It is the lack of them that has led to it."

"I have forbidden that talk. You appear not to follow simple speech. I will make it simpler. I will not have the word mentioned."

"What word?" said Ralph.

"Do you need me to tell you?"

"You should be able to. You have not scrupled to use it. And we owe it to you."

"The workhouse," said Sir Edwin, smiling. "The talk of it has amused me."

"I fear it has been meant to," said Simon. "It has become conscious talk; indeed we must say self-conscious. You are too kind to them."

"Well, I am living a last scene. I am preparing a memory. I must be allowed to be at my best."

"You have not to erase other memories," said Fanny. "Your task is not a hard one."

"Edwin," said Julia, "—I am the last person to call you that, and have you do the same to me—if you meet my Hamish, you will tell him all I should wish? You know what it is. I need not use the words."

"I will tell him, if I meet him."

"But you do not think you will, sir?" said Ralph.

"No one can be sure," said Julia.

"We can be; we are," said Sir Edwin. "You mean we may be wrong."

"Is this a good choice of subject?" said Simon, to his son.

"It was not I who introduced it."

"I am glad not to feel I shall meet people," said Graham. "Fancy meeting someone when you had lost his letters, or lost what he left you, through trying to increase it, when it was enough, and you had no right to it! I should find it too much."

"I should like to meet everyone," said Walter. "I should not dream of doing such things. I am wonderful with people's memories. I am glad for Uncle to know it."

"Yes, we are here to think only of him," said Simon.

"Graham had not mentioned himself before," said Fanny.

"It was more than a mention then."

"Why are we supposed to take so little interest in ourselves?" said Naomi. "I suppose people can't believe we can take any. And of course we do have to hide it."

"If you remember my wish, Edwin, I will say no more," said Julia.

"I will remember, as long as I have a memory."

"And that will be during your life here," said Ralph, glancing at his father.

"So I must see Hamish before it ends. I shall carry nothing with me."

"He should be here at any hour," said Rhoda. "It may be at this one."

"We will all go and leave you with him," said Simon.

"No, you will stay," said Sir Edwin, leaning forward and laying his hand on his, as if to hold him. "You must hear my words and remember them. You know what they will be. I must leave Hamish in my place, and feel he will fill it. I want to trust you and him. The truth of this moment depends on the truth to come."

"I understand you, Uncle. You may trust me."

"I will not say more before he is here. My strength is not much, and is ebbing. I am wise to save it."

"Are we all to be here, sir?" said Graham.

"All of you who will stay. It secures my purpose."

"Any behest of yours is safe with us, Edwin," said Julia. "That is why I feel that mine is with you."

Fanny was looking at Naomi, knowing her thought.

"You would like to go, my dear? I would come with you."

"No, I can be here, as Hamish will be. We can both do what we must."

"There is the carriage!" said Rhoda. "I was listening for it. I sent it to meet the later train, in case Hamish was on it. It joins the train from the coast. Yes, he is there! I hear him."

Hamish's voice came across the hall in greeting to Deakin.

"Mr. Hamish!" said the latter at the door.

"Why, everyone is here! Mother, it is good to see you. Father, I am glad to be with you again. I have made all the haste I could——"

"To be in time," said Sir Edwin. "It was the thing to do. I am further downhill than you knew, nearly at the bottom.

But it is my place, and I am easy in it. The hill has been a long one. You will be with me, as I go to the end."

"I will always be with you, Father. How are you, Aunt Fanny and Aunt Julia? And Naomi and all of you? I am glad to be amongst you again. I am not happy away from my place. I find it is mine."

"Exile has done its work," said Sir Edwin. "It has taught you what you had to learn. There is to be some meaning in our years together. It is an old man's wish, to leave his difference behind. But an old man is what I am."

"It will be as you say, Uncle," said Simon, "as we all see it, would all choose it to be. It is not an old or a young man's wish. It is the wish of us all."

"So I look at the years ahead, and see them as you will live them. But, Hamish, I want your word on it, your promise that you will take my place, to the best that is in you, to the end of your days. I have been waiting for it. And I should not wait too long."

"I am to give it, Cousin Simon?" said Hamish, lowering his voice and just glancing at Simon. "I know this is how you wished it to be, that you would not accept my other word. You said you would wait for me to unsay it. You spoke the truth, as you seemed to speak it? I know you are what you seem to be. I am to give my father my promise?"

"You are to give it. I need not say again what I have said."

"I promise it, Father," said Hamish. "I will do my best. There is much that is beyond me, but I will try to reach it. And I am not to be without support."

"So our great-uncle goes in peace," murmured Ralph. "And Father is to stay where he is. He seems to be prepared for it. But he was also prepared for something else."

"Hamish has suffered a sea change," said Graham. "Into something that is strange, if nothing more. It has come of his travels. But I am not sure what it is."

"Nor am I," said Naomi. "Though I saw it in a moment, heard it in his first word. But we shall soon know."

They were not to know at once. That evening Sir Edwin

was weaker, and in the hour before daybreak he died. Rhoda and Hamish and Deakin were with him. The meeting and its questions had told on him, and they knew it and were at hand. He died with the ease of his great age, and it seemed more of a change than a grief. He had let them feel his life was past.

It was not until after the burial, that the families met in Hamish's house.

"So you are our head now, Hamish," said Julia. "You are in your father's place—in the—the place that falls to you. You will find it a great change."

"We are haunted by double meanings," said Ralph to Naomi. "They hover about us."

"No one else would speak of it," said Simon, in a low, sharp tone. "Where is the need to do so?"

"This day brings another back to me," said Julia. "The day when my husband was buried, Edwin's younger brother! All those years ago! Life is a strange thing. It will soon be my turn to follow."

"What ought we to say?" said Graham. "Silence means consent, and seems to mean it. And yet we can hardly disagree."

"Say nothing," said Simon.

"Father is in a sinister mood," said Ralph. "It can hardly be the loss of his uncle at ninety-four."

"You know what it is," said Graham. "You are not the one of us in doubt. When Grandma used ambiguous words, you caught their meaning."

"As she did," said Ralph. "It is true that the meaning was there."

"I am always happy in my old home," said Julia, looking round. "It is the one house I know, where the present has not ousted the past. Everything is as it has been and will be. We can trust Hamish."

"I would alter nothing of my own purpose, Aunt Julia. But I may be too sunk in the old tradition to judge. We can be too sure that the future can teach us nothing."

"I think the past does more for us," said Simon, looking at him. "It gives what has lasted, and so can continue to last."

"Cousin Simon, the present has given me something. Something I did not think to have again. Something to take the place of what I lost. I hoped to tell my father, while you all heard me. It is in its way a hard thing for me to tell. But the moment was not good for him, and now is past. I move into a future he did not foresee. But we cannot stay where he left us. We must all go forward."

There was a pause.

"You are going to be married!" said Graham. "I knew there was a difference. I had a—foreboding is not the word. You have the good wishes of us all."

"My son!" said Rhoda. "What have you from your mother? Her promise of welcome, her joy in yielding her place. Ah, indeed you have it."

"It is a piece of news indeed," said Julia. "The surprise is almost too great. It is the last thing we thought of. We had been involved in different things."

"This adds itself to them. It makes my life into a whole. I can look both back and forward and see so much."

"It helped you with your promise to your father. Yes, we see that it did. You are glad to succeed him, and have so much to give. That is how you see the matter again. We understand it, and wish you well from our hearts."

"That is what I should say," said Walter, in a low tone to Simon, "if I dared to say it, if it would not mean too much from me. And it would mean it all."

"My wife and I are glad for you, Hamish," said Simon. "Marriage is for most of us the best thing."

"Naomi, you are glad for me? Glad for yourself to have the help in banishing the past? For we have to forget it. This can be the last word."

"Yes, I am glad," said Naomi.

"I am not," muttered Ralph. "I shall be a cynic for life. I suppose it had to be. There is the cynicism beginning.

But it should not have been so soon. Cynicism cannot go too far. Hamish says it is his nature to be led. He need not say it again to me."

"Naomi," said Graham, "I wished the truth need not be told, that you and Hamish could marry. I feel I do not wish it now."

"I saw the change. I saw and felt it from the first. Hamish thinks it will help me to forget. Of course it makes me remember. It is the change in him that will help me. And seeing it is not really a change."

"I wish my father had lived to know," said Hamish, looking round with the ease of confession past. "To know that his line would be continued, and to meet the woman who would do it. But I feel that perhaps he does know."

"His very beliefs are different," said Ralph. "He was a sceptic when he left us. The change goes right through him."

"He is what he was," said Naomi. "He is not a person to be always the same. He took his colour from us, and we could not know it was our own. It is we who have changed. We have come to a knowledge of him."

"We can find no excuse for people who let us have that?" said Walter. "They would not deserve one."

"If a thing needs excuse, it naturally cannot have it," said Graham.

"Hamish wished your uncle had lived to know this, Simon," said Fanny. "What do you feel yourself?"

"That I am glad he did not know."

"I am worse than you. I am wishing he had known, and showed his feeling. And I was grateful to your mother for her speech."

"I think you are to have further cause for gratitude."

"We begin to follow it all, Hamish," said Julia. "We see why you inclined to put the future above the past. It was so unlike you, that we were struck by it. I hope your wife will respect our old order. But I have no doubt she will."

"We must not expect her to accept it, as if it were hers.

151

She will put her own mark on things. It is what I want and ask of her."

"And you wished your father had lived to know it?" said Julia, in a fainter tone.

"It is raining," said Fanny, quickly. "And the children are in the garden. Miss Dolton went to the village, and left them to play outside."

"They must come in," said Hamish, going to the window and beckoning. "It is raining fast. Come up to the fire, both of you. I hope you are not wet?"

"Well, we are," said Claud. "We have been out in the rain."

"We stood by the wall," said Emma. "It was the sensible thing to do."

"Well, now you must get dry, and hear my news. You will not guess what it is."

"I expect we shall," said Claud. "We often guess. You are going to marry Naomi, after all."

"No, but I am going to marry someone. Someone whom you will come to love. It is great news, isn't it?"

"Well, we don't mind about it. Why is it great? Why can you marry her, when you couldn't marry Naomi?"

"Well, she and I are not cousins."

"Why do you want so much to marry? You have two people to live with."

"He only has one now," said Emma.

"Well, it is a thing you will want yourself one day."

"I want it now. I want to marry Emma. But I am too young by the law."

"Well, Emma must refuse to marry anyone else."

"I think a father can make a girl marry anyone he likes. I know he used to be able to. And it was—it was a father, who would not let you and Naomi marry, though of course there was a reason."

"Well, history need not repeat itself," said Simon, smiling or giving a smile. "I will not make Emma marry anyone."

"Nor forbid her to marry me?" said Claud, on a faintly incredulous note.

"No, I will not do that either."

"You are very fond of Emma," said Julia. "That is a great thing for you both."

"Yes, I am dependent on her. I find her a support."

"Yes, he does," said Emma. "He has to lean on some-one."

"Then he is like me," said Hamish.

"No, I don't think I am," said Claud, at once. "When I depend on a person, I couldn't ever have anyone instead."

"No, he couldn't," said Emma. "He has a faithful heart. It is the only thing worth having."

"It has stopped raining," said Fanny, as if she felt this to be fortunate. "You may run out again."

"We don't need to run," said Claud, as he walked to the door. "We shall get out soon enough. We will go on with our game."

"What are you playing at?" said Julia.

"We are Father and Uncle Walter in their old haunts. This used to be their garden. I am Uncle, and Emma is Father."

"Why, it should be the other way round. You are the elder."

"Yes, but only a year. And Emma takes the lead."

"Yes, I do," said his sister. "But I don't try to be what Father was. It must seem to us that he has never been a child."

"So it would be no good to copy him," said Claud.

"And we don't copy people," said Emma. "We know where that would lead."

"Shut the door," called Simon after them. "No, do not shut it for them, Fanny. Let Claud do it himself."

"I am glad to have it between them and us," said his wife, as she achieved this.

"Tell us all you have to tell, Hamish," said Graham. "We have hardly learned much yet."

"You shall know it all. I hope you will soon know her. It is to be such a good friendship. I have thought of it all the time. I met her by chance. She is older than I am, but not enough to matter, if such a thing could count to me, as it could not. She is gifted and widely read, my superior in every sense. She has no parents, and is independent in means, and very independent in herself. I need not describe her. You will soon do so yourselves. I long to see her and Naomi together. It should be something that will last their lives."

"So Hamish is providing compensation for Naomi," said Ralph. "And in a form he might not have thought of."

"Claud said it was not great news," said Rhoda, in a quiet tone, "But to me it was."

"Mother, it was the most to you. It is a thing that goes without saying."

"The news itself did not do so."

"We will leave you to discuss it, Rhoda," said Simon. "It was your right to know before anyone. Hamish must render his account."

"It seemed best to tell you all at once, Cousin Simon. And you made it easy for me. I shall not forget it."

"There was no reason to make it hard for you," said Simon, as they left the house.

"There was," said Walter. "But we could not act upon it. Why is it compulsory to be so virtuous?"

"I ought not to say it," said Julia. "But shall we think the same of Hamish? After all he said, when he knew his first wish must be denied him?"

"Well, it was his first," said Graham. "We can remember that."

"I suppose he could not be expected never to marry."

"He could for the time," said Ralph. "It was what we did expect."

"Never is a long word," said Walter. "And the time since the truth was known, is short."

"It may be best for the change to come," said Ralph. "It

saves Naomi from trying to be her old self, when things are different. But what is best and what is good are not the same."

"It is Hamish himself who surprises us," said Julia. "We must say it is."

"We do no good by continuing to say it," said Simon.

"I get great help from it," said Walter. "And more from hearing it said. Our mothers are our best comforters. They are not ashamed of being openly what we all are underneath."

"Their exemption from criticism gives them courage," said Graham. "And then they get more and more exempt. No one dares to begin it. Things have gone too far."

"Nothing has given me courage," said Fanny. "I have never felt more without it."

"You could hardly have it in your place as Naomi's mother," said Simon, in a quiet tone.

"My son, I think of what you feel as her father," said Julia.

"This is what I feel," said Simon, putting an arm about his daughter. "She and I suffer the same thing. We are both debarred from our place. Each of us might have had it or seen the other in it. Neither of us will do so now. We might each have had much or something. Now we simply have each other."

"So Naomi's experience is matched by his," muttered Ralph.

"That is what is said, when people have sustained some loss," said Graham. "As if they had not had each other all the time! It is hard to accept it as a recompense."

"This position that our great-uncle had!" said Ralph. "That Father and Naomi might have had. That you in your turn would have had. That Hamish actually has! It has had to go a long way. No wonder things have not gone well. I have moved on alone towards the familiar goal. I somehow feel surprised by it."

"Then be silent about it," said Simon. "We have all in a way retraced our steps."

"There will be a certain zest in going forward," said Julia. "In knowing Hamish's wife, and seeing their life together. We cannot say there will not."

"Why should we want to say it?" said Walter. "It is the thing we have to sustain us."

"If we were without it, we should not want it," said Graham. "The truth creates its own need."

Simon turned to his wife.

"I begin to feel almost glad I had to tell the truth. Hamish has become an uncertain figure. I feel I have not known him. And I think I see he has not known any of us."

"Or he would not have made his confession at so little cost. We had to feel it was less than it might have been."

"It is hard to forgive it," said Walter. "I shall not even try."

"We might say we had nothing to forgive," said Fanny. "But it is a thing we seldom say, if it is true."

"Hamish has betrayed himself," said Graham. "I wonder if he knows it. His letting his mother hear the news with all of us! And the way she accepted it! It does throw its light."

"There was no need of it on her," said Julia. "Everything comes of the one thing. She has felt she has no right to her motherhood, no claim on him as a son. Her secret was the cause of it."

"Do you make it explain more than is there?" said Simon.

"No," said Fanny. "She sees what it is. My sister changed after her marriage, it may have been at that time. Up to a point it must have been."

"Well, we are at home," said Ralph. "In the house that is that to us, until we leave it for the other. We know it for certain now."

"Did you mean the grave or the workhouse?" said Simon, in a changed tone. "Tell me the truth."

"That—the grave," said Ralph, not doing this.

Emma emerged from the bushes.

"You forgot to bring us home."

"Oh, we did!" said Fanny. "Other things drove it from our minds. How did you get here?"

"Miss Dolton fetched us after you had gone. She thought you might forget. You didn't even see us on the road."

"I daresay not," said Ralph. "We had things to talk about."

"Well, everyone has. It was funny that seven people forgot. It was nine, if you count Aunt Rhoda and Hamish. But they were not responsible."

"It was certainly remiss," said Graham.

"What does that mean?"

"Neglectful of something that ought to be done."

"Yes, it is exactly the word, isn't it?"

Claud appeared beside his sister.

"We were left in the other garden. We might almost have been orphans."

"I wonder how you would feel, if you were," said Simon. "You would not overlook the difference."

"It might not be very much. We should still have Miss Dolton."

"Not if you were orphans. There would be no home for you or her."

"It didn't really seem as if there was."

"You could have gone into the other house."

"Not unless we were asked," said Emma. "We have no claim on people, because we are children. It does not do to think along that line."

"Hamish could have brought you home," said Fanny.

"He didn't think of it. And we could hardly expect him to. He has become a stranger to us, hasn't he?"

# CHAPTER XII

"Mother, here she is!" said Hamish. "Here, where she is to be, where she and I are to be old together, where you will see us grow into our full selves! Our last, long chapter has begun."

"And must go on," said his wife, as she shook hands with Rhoda and glanced into her face. "And I have not had a wedding or appeared in any proper light. I have indeed not appeared at all. I am seen at once as a stranger and a son's wife."

"I want things as they are, and her as she is," said Hamish. "I would not have anything different."

"But I daresay your mother would," said his wife, looking aside, as she hurried the words she had to say. "I am eleven years older than you, and full of opinions, they say, though most of us have them, and it might be no better to have none. Anyhow she sees me, such as I am; and for myself alone I would be a thousand times more fair, but perhaps no more rich, as it would not become me to have much."

"I am thirty-nine years older than Hamish," said Rhoda, as the rapid, deep tones ceased. "I shall see you become your full selves. You will see me fall away from mine."

"I am myself now. Nothing is to come. You must take me as I am, as people say. As though that justified their being what they are, when probably nothing could!"

"This is the dining-room," said Rhoda, leading the way across the hall. "I daresay you guessed it would be here."

"I was wondering if it was anywhere, the hall was so wide. It has had a long history as what it is. How many people have sat here at a time?"

"Ah, many in the past. Very few sit here now. But our family from the other house will be with us to-night; Hamish's two older cousins and their mother, and the elder one's wife, who is my sister, and their sons and daughter. Then we shall be ten at the table, many for us now. But everyone is too anxious to know you to be left behind."

"It is the daughter, whom Hamish would have married, if he could? I wonder if she does want to meet me. I want to meet her, though I shall have to feel humble in her eyes."

"Marcia knows everything, Mother," said Hamish. "I had nothing in my life to hide. And I did not make a mystery of this one thing, that was not my fault. It would have been a precarious secret. And the truth does all that needs to be done."

"I would not have spoken of it," said Marcia, keeping her eyes from Rhoda's face, "except to let you know that I knew. It seemed you had to know."

Rhoda answered at once.

"It has been so much to follow from so little. That is how I must see it. It is all I can say."

"It is the thing to be said," said Marcia, turning her eyes about the room. "It seems as if nothing had ever been altered here. I suppose nothing has."

"Do you want to alter anything?" said Hamish.

"I could not think of it. Nothing could be different. It would be like changing something unearthed after ages. The time for it is past."

"Don't you like it as it is?"

"I like it in itself, but hardly for me. It does not offer me anything."

"You will grow into it and become a part of it," said Rhoda. "That is what our women do."

"It will draw me into itself. I felt it would."

"You would like something modern?" said Hamish.

"No, but something lighter and more on my level. And I don't mean the level is low, or that I shall think of it. I am answering your questions."

"When I was a boy, I felt as you do, or should have, if I had thought it possible. But I have learned to like it and live with it. You will do the same."

"You have a long start. And time is longer in youth."

"I am part of the lesson Hamish has learned," said Rhoda. "I hope you can do as well as he."

"I am glad to have someone to balance his youth and cover my lack of it. I feel less of a husk, with everything worn away." Marcia glanced round the room, as though finding her words in tune with it.

"Hamish will show you the house. He feels it is his to give to you."

"She does not want it," said Hamish, looking at his wife. "She is as yet a stranger to it. But she will come to share it with me."

"You may have the whole. I shall not see any part as mine. I will deal with it as something to pass on, as it came into my hands. Neither better nor worse; it would be wrong for it to be either. As we change, it will not change with us. It is like some fossilised thing, that has come to withstand time. That is what it is."

"You will soon see living people here, my aunts and my cousins of two generations. You know we call them what they are thought to be."

"Do you feel they are seen as that?" said Marcia, as they went upstairs.

"If they are not, we shall never know. We do not mean ever to know. The truth is to be covered by silence, and gradually by time. That is what my father used to say."

"No wonder you were tempted to say it. I hope it will be as good as it sounds. It seems the way to speak in this house. And it is right that it should have a secret. It is not such a sinister one. Did your cousin mind his disinheritance, when you were born?"

"More than he has said, or thought I knew. More than I knew anyone could mind anything, that was not a grief. I suppose that is what it was. He loves the place more than I do, more than my father did, more than my mother has come to. He has cared for it better than I could. I am wise to leave it in his hands."

"Your mother does not mind your marrying. You have not been everything to each other."

"No, not as you mean it. There has been a lack of emotion in our life. You know enough to understand."

"I am glad not to exact a sacrifice. That sounds of more advantage than it is. Of course we don't have the chance to get used to it. I daresay it is a taste we could acquire."

"This is to be our room," said Hamish. "It is the one my father had. My mother has never slept here. She has the one that was his brother's."

"I ought to be different," said Marcia, turning to the glass, to see her tall, spare figure, low, wide brow, deep-set grey eyes and straight, unyouthful features as strangers would see them. "I am older and plainer and less poor than I ought to be. Someone younger and more dependent would fit the part. And the house would have more welcome for her."

"My mother likes you, I can see," said Hamish.

"And do you see that I like her? How well do you know me? It is not the people I am afraid of here, but the place. I shall be glad to feel it is inhabited by human beings like myself, though they might not so describe themselves. I feel that you and I and your mother might be immured here and forgotten."

"There is no lack of family life. I hope it will not be too much."

"Better that than too little, anyhow better than nothing. We must have something more than emptiness."

The hour came when the other family entered the house. Marcia faced the seven pairs of eyes with their interest and question of the future, and responded, as she did everything, according to herself. When she had glanced once from Hamish's face to Simon's, she did not do so again.

"This is a new day for us," said Fanny. "The history

of our house unfolds. It is a thing that is serious to us. My sister and I have learned it."

"I am learning," said Marcia. "I have already gone a little way. It is hard to look at the future of a place with so much behind. It seems that such a long history must be near its end. I shall need help."

"You shall have it," said Simon. "And you will not want it long. It is a grateful house, kind to its inmates, sad to lose them. When I left it, I felt its sympathy, and I still feel it."

"I knew it was human. I must simply resist its hold. I cannot be bound and burdened. I must be free and travel light. I shall live in it, an alien, in the end I daresay a slave, but never drawn into it, always apart in myself."

"I could be away from it for fifty years and never be apart."

"I could be in it for as long, and always be. My hope is to fear and serve it, and hand it on to people who love the bond. I could never join them."

"The wives of our family have done so. It has gone on through the centuries."

"As everything has here," said Marcia, as they went in to dinner. "Nothing belongs to the present, and it is in the present that we live. Otherwise we live in what is not there, in what is in our minds and nowhere else. I must go forward and not back. We know what is behind. What is before us is enough."

"What is behind is a part of us, rooted in our being. We have grown from it. Something deep in us remembers it. In a sense nothing is forgotten."

"In another sense everything is. And nothing in me remembers this. Everything warns me that I am to take nothing from it, and give it myself. Well, it has taken better people, and will take more."

"Different people, we will say," said Simon.

"Another institution is to receive us in the end," said Ralph. "We are glad to feel we can rely on it."

"The workhouse?" said Marcia, smiling at once. "It is far removed from this one. But I believe the past rules there as well. So you may in a way be prepared for it."

"This subject already!" said Simon. "You must forgive my son. He has no other."

"It was my father who introduced it. And he has not provided a second."

"Hamish's birth upset a great deal," said Marcia to Simon, and paused.

"It was a natural change. One that often happens," said Simon, and also paused.

"You must not think we did not welcome Hamish," said Julia, from her place.

"No one could have welcomed me," said Hamish to his wife. "Certainly the house did not. Of course my mother did in time. Yes, I am to sit opposite Cousin Simon, on your other side. Graham is taking my place. I am to have my own way tonight."

Marcia lowered her tone.

"Hamish, I wish you had not told me. I wish I did not know. No one can speak or be spoken to, without saying or hearing too much. How is it all to go on, and how to end?"

"I had to tell you. You had to know about Naomi. You would have seen in time."

"I could have thought you had broken things off in some other way. It is a common thing."

"How long would you have thought it? You would have seen and heard. You are not a person who does not do both. And I did not break it off. I should not have done so. I would not let anyone think it. Least of all would I let you. What would you think of me? What should I think of myself?"

"Yes, I see I had to know. And the knowledge in itself is nothing. It is the mystery and meaning that smother it. But I shall do my part. It is an easier one than yours."

"Hamish and I have ended our feeling," said Naomi.

"The sense of our relationship helped us. It is true that we needed help."

"And I thought I had little in my life," said Hamish, looking from one to the other. "Now I have both of you, I feel it is so much."

"I wish I had less," said Marcia, smiling. "All this that surrounds me, and all these relations who are something else! It stretches over the future."

"And we seem a fated family," said Ralph. "Claud is resolved to marry Emma. And we must admit it is on our line."

"I am sorry for such talk," said Simon. "I should have thought my son would know better."

"You surely had not such a hope of me, sir."

"It is true that I am hardly given it."

"I wish you had never had to leave this house," said Marcia to Simon. "I wish it could have been different. It seems it might have been. Hamish could not be your son, and yet had to be, when his life denied it. It is a hard, sad thing. And it came from so little."

"The last word is a true and kind one."

"It is the only one. How often you have said it!"

"We must not say it again. The truth is not to be thought or said. It is as if it had not been."

"You know it is not. It will never be. It might be so more, if we were not all here together, if Hamish and I were somewhere else. It is Hamish who forces it to the surface, so that it follows us with all that must be hidden. And the cloud is lasting. It will never lift."

"It all seems to settle into something we accept and do not question. We learn to live with it."

"Because for you there is no escape. You are bound to this place, that shadows you with a dead past and a threatened future. But as I am added to your other women, I suffer something more than they. I can never send my roots down here, only move on the surface, uneasy and aloof. It is so much less than they have given."

"It is a good deal from you," said Simon. "It would come to be more. And Hamish promised his father to take his place."

"He had made an earlier promise. That claim is the first."

"I could not accept it. I waited for it to be withdrawn. I was glad when it was."

"You were glad to allow it to be, to do what you owed to yourself, feeling you owed more, because of the one betrayal. That is not gladness."

"It was the kind I could have. The other was not for me. I have only the right to forget it. Here are the children come to greet you, before they go to bed. Come and say 'how-do-you-do?' to Cousin Marcia."

"Is she really our cousin?" said Claud.

"She is your cousin by marriage. That is what you will call her."

"I don't expect we shall call her anything," said Emma. "You can speak to people without a name."

"I shall know whom you mean," said Marcia. "Am I what you thought I should be?"

"Well, you are older," said Claud. "And taller and not like Naomi. When you are really instead of her, it is strange for you to be so different."

"It might seem that Hamish couldn't like both of you," said Emma. "But of course we know he did."

"No one is instead of anyone else," said Julia. "Everyone has his own place."

"Don't you mean *her* place?" said Claud. "There was really only one for both of them. Unless one of them was a concubine, and we know they weren't that. Then he might have had hundreds."

"I don't think he might," said Emma. "Solomon was a king."

"Are you glad that Hamish has given you this house?" said Claud. "He was going to give it to Naomi. But as she didn't marry him, there is nothing unfair."

"I think it is too large and old a house for me."

"It is not what you are used to," said Emma, in sympathy. "We never want to stay in it. Though it is better than an orphanage would be."

"Well, you may leave it," said Simon. "And your nurse is waiting. So say good-night and run away."

"Why do people say 'run', when they don't mean it?" said Claud. "Must we say good-night to everyone at the table?"

"No, only to Cousin Marcia and Grandma and Mother."

"Shan't we say it to Uncle Walter? He is getting old."

"Well, you can say it to him, though he is younger than I am."

"But you are giving the directions," said Emma. "So you would not say anything was due to yourself."

"Why were they thinking of an orphanage?" said Marcia.

"We all have to think of an alternative shelter," said Ralph. "We are not to depend on our present one."

"Oh, it corresponds to the workhouse at their age."

"These are boyish young men," said Simon, as they rose from the table.

"They scarcely seem so," said Marcia. "The thought of the workhouse has come soon. In youth it is an end for other people."

"Not in our youth," said Ralph.

Marcia glanced at Simon's face and said no more.

"You see it all," said Hamish, moving to her. "My birth dispossessed Cousin Simon and broke up his future. And my promise to withdraw on my father's death changed things and gave it back to him. But he accepted my later word to my father, and wished me to keep it, indeed looked for the change. And he knows he caused his displacement himself, and has no grievance."

"So it means so much to him?" said Marcia. "Does Graham feel the same?"

"He might, if he allowed himself to. But he sees things as they are."

"Your cousin does too, and cannot bear the sight. You do not love the place as they do?"

"Not as much. My mother did not help me. She has hardly felt at home in the house, or felt it to be her home. She found it as you do, oppressive to a stranger. But you will cease to be so. Cousin Simon will help you. I think he has begun."

Marcia looked at Simon's tall, set figure, dark, grave eyes and firm, controlled face, and looked again about her.

"This is his place," she said. "It is time he had it. And it is not for him. That is his tragedy. That is the reason of the talk of the workhouse and the orphanage, and the jests that have something behind them. His family is not where it should be, or should have been; he is not there."

Walter came up to Marcia.

"Do you like sitting in your place at table, and displacing Hamish's mother? I ask because I want to know. It is not petty curiosity. Petty is the last word. It is great and deep."

"I like it no more than she does. I daresay less. I don't want to be there, or anywhere under this roof. I wonder how anyone comes to rest beneath it. What is your feeling?"

"To me it is my background. Coming here is coming home. I see my brother as the head, and Hamish as a herald of the future, come to it out of due time."

"I see it as you do, and Hamish as you see him. This home in the past has no meaning for me. I want to have one I can hold and help to grow. The time for it had come, and I let it pass. And Hamish in his heart is with me. I am doing him no service."

"Your position here will give you something of its own."

"Perhaps it will, but I would choose something else. I am not proud of being the mistress here. I see no cause for pride. I see Hamish's mother unseated, and know I may be myself one day. I have no roots here, no rights here, only the right of occupation and service until my use is past. Hamish himself has nothing here except on a life tenure. It is not enough for us, just as it is too much. And his father would be in his place, fulfilled and useful, ready to yield it in his time in the way the past has sanctified. Which is the better thing?"

"You must not speak of my brother as Hamish's father."

"It is how I think of him, how you know I do. His supposed father is only a name to me. And in some ways he was to Hamish only a name."

"He came to be more. And Hamish promised at his deathbed to take his place."

"Another promise came first. Which is it better to break? One must be broken."

"You would not suggest that Hamish should transfer the place to my brother?"

"It would not be my suggestion. It was his own. I would suggest that he should keep his first word."

"My brother would not accept it. He is what he is. He would not live except on terms with his conscience."

"He makes his own terms," said Marcia, smiling. "He can cast a gloom over his family, show them a warped outlook and expect another, because of his own frustration. So he could surely mend matters by accepting a promise, that stood by itself. The second could not really be given."

"He does not know he does what you say. Of course, I do not deny it."

"He would be different in his own sphere. He once was different."

"How do you know it?"

Marcia did not reply.

"He knows that things will go down through Hamish to his own descendants," said Walter.

"He knows it and cannot feel it. Just as he knows and cannot feel that Hamish is his son. Just as Hamish knows and cannot feel it. The long darkness has deprived the truth of its life."

"You and my brother would make a good pair," said

Walter, looking from one to the other. "One could think of another story."

Marcia was again silent.

"Are you talking about me?" said Simon, coming up to them. "I keep feeling your eyes upon me."

"Yes," said Marcia, as Walter moved away. "I was picturing you in this house as its head, and the transmitter of it to your line. You are better fitted for it than Hamish, readier to serve it selflessly, with your eyes on the future you will not see. You would give it yourself, as you would give it to nothing else. Hamish could give himself to many things. He gave himself to Naomi; he has given himself to me. You have yourself to give. Hamish's promise to you came first. There was no truth in the second. He gave it under pressure at a deathbed. He was helpless and cannot be blamed. But neither can he be held to it. One promise must be broken. Which should it be?"

"The promise to me means nothing. I did not accept it."

"Let us forget the promises. Neither means much, as there are more than one. Let us see my idea in itself."

"Is it right or wrong?" said Simon. "It is not right because it serves us, or even serves others."

"Let it be neither," said Marcia. "We will not say it is right. But its serving us and others does not make it wrong. And many would be served."

"My family?" said Simon. "That need not count. I would anyhow do better there."

"Then you and I and Hamish. Who is better for the other decision?"

"No one," said Simon, after a pause.

"Then what is there to balance our gain?"

"Nothing."

"Then consider if you are feeling it wrong, because it serves yourself. That is a common snare. And it is putting ourselves too high."

There was a pause.

"You have not said anything to Hamish?"

"Not yet; there is no need; a word will be enough. He will live with me anywhere, and his mother will live with us. Neither has a heart in the place. Have you your heart in it?"

There was a long silence.

"You said I should serve it selflessly," said Simon, "with my eyes on the future that I should not see. That is how I will serve it. And you are right that there is nothing else, to which I have given myself. I might in another state of things, with times and ages different, have given myself to someone. That is a thought that may return."

"There is one that will be with me. That my children will be your grandchildren. It will sometimes be with you. When other people forget it, we shall not."

"Look at Father and Marcia standing together," said Graham to his sister. "They seem an essential man and woman, like some pair in history or art. They ought to be sculptured or painted and handed down to posterity."

Marcia and Simon were joined by Hamish, and the three stood in talk. Then Rhoda and Fanny were summoned, and a few words sent the history of the house into another channel. Later the sisters moved to each other.

"So you are to live in the house, and I am to leave it," said Rhoda. "Which of us is fortunate?"

"Neither of us," said Fanny, as if the words escaped her. "We have known the place and served it. We have seen it regarded as something it could not be. As a force in the background, with human lives helpless in the fore. And that is not what it is. It may be so in some minds; in Simon's, perhaps in Graham's; not in yours or mine. We have not had good fortune."

"You must be glad that Simon's life is to be fulfilled, before it is too late."

"It is too late. For his family, if not for him. It might not be, if he had borne things better, cared more for his son; I feel it, though Hamish is not mine; had not wreaked on helpless creatures in his power the frustration he had brought on himself. That cannot be altered or forgotten. It is too late."

"How will Walter see the change?"

"As the restoration of Simon to his place. That is what it means to him. And the credit is due to Simon."

"You have been happy with Simon, Fanny?"

"Yes, he has been a good husband, a fair partner in life. He likes and is kind to women. You know how he felt to you. He has never failed in affection for me. And you saw him with Marcia; for a moment, but it was enough. He is on one side of him a gentle, normal man. And I have never been tempted to say he is an ordinary one."

"I saw him with Marcia. That is, I saw them together. They are not to be so; we are to live elsewhere; I see it will be best. As you say, a moment was enough."

"I like your son's wife, Rhoda. You will like her too."

"I shall come to love her. I see she will love me. But Hamish is young, and she had the other thing before her eyes. She will have it in her thought. She has seen Simon at his best, and his best is what you say. You will have more of it now. You will find him different."

"Yes, and so we can be. But we shall see him being so, and shall be the same. It is we who will cast the cloud. But he will not suffer from it; he will not see it; his own prospect will be clear. You think I am talking bitterly. I am speaking the truth. The truth can sometimes be bitter."

Simon went up to Hamish and spoke without looking at him.

"We shall always feel it, Hamish. In keeping one promise you break the other. It is a thing we take with us."

"I could not keep both, sir. And I could not help the second. And my life has changed, and everything has changed with it. I lived with my eyes on the past, and did not see it. Now I must think of the future, and watch it coming. I found someone to help me, when my mother and I needed help. I shall not mind living on my wife's means, as she wished me to give up my own. You have yielded to me, seeing it was best. I am grateful to you in a way you cannot be to me. If we are grateful in any way to each other, it is a good thing to feel, as our roads part. And the roads will cross at times.—It is time for you to go? It will not be you, who leave the house, when we meet here again. Good-night and thank you, Cousin Simon."

"I will say now what I must not say then," said Simon. "Good-night and thank you, my son."

# CHAPTER XIII

"Well, how do you like the new home?" said Simon, entering the nursery.

"It is your old home, isn't it?" said Claud. "You always say it is."

"Well, it is new to you."

"It is not new," said Emma, looking round. "It couldn't be that to anyone."

"You know it is a very old house, that has been in our family for centuries."

"Does that mean hundreds of years?" said Claud. "But hundreds are not thousands."

"It doesn't go back to the Druids," said Emma.

"Well, would it be better, if it did?"

"It would be older. And so people would think it was."

"But you like everything to be new?" said Simon.

"Well, new things cost more money," said Claud. "And people would not pay it without a cause."

"It is all a question of money in the end," said Emma, lifting her shoulders.

"Well, what do you think of your new—your nursery?" said Simon.

"It is large and rather dark," said Claud.

"You like it to be large surely?"

"In a way. But it is quite a walk between the cupboard and the fire."

"And space beyond a point only means work," said Emma.

"Come, do not quote other people. I asked you how you liked the room."

"You asked what we thought of it," said Claud. "You

must not mind, if we tell you. And I said it was rather dark. It is not so very."

"The corners are dark," said Emma. "There might be —you might think there were things in them, if you didn't know."

"She means in the evening, before we have the light," said Claud. "And of course there isn't anything. You can see it the next day."

"How do Nurse and Miss Dolton like the room?"

"Well, they find it eerie," said Emma, sighing. "People are only what they are."

"How about the rooms you sleep in? Do you like those better?"

"Oh, yes," said Emma, in a generous tone. "They are just ordinary rooms."

"They are in the modern wing. What strange tastes you all have!"

"They can't be strange, if we all have them. It may be yours that are that. It is the word for this house, and you grew up in it."

"It is almost more than a house," said Claud. "It is really not itself without a drawbridge."

"But then there would have to be a moat," said his father.

"Well, one could be made. A moat would have to be dug. It is not there of itself."

"It is not a natural feature," said Emma.

"I know what you mean," said Simon, not out of sympathy with the view. "But a moat was made to keep out enemies. And there is none here."

"It might keep out other things," said Emma. "Everything is not human."

"You are not thinking of ghosts, are you?"

"I wasn't thinking of anything in particular."

"Thoughts need not be exact," said Claud, as Simon left them.

"I have a pair of odd children," said the latter, as he

joined his family. "Emma and Claud find their nursery too much for them. When I feel they are at last in their home."

"The question of homes is always ominous for us," said Ralph.

"And it dies hard," said his father, smiling. "Indeed I see it will never die."

"Has anyone heard from the exiles?" said Julia.

"I have a letter from Rhoda," said Fanny. "She does not see herself in that light. She and her young couple are happy in their new home. They are not like Claud and Emma."

"Or rather they are," said Graham. "They do not feel the spell of this one."

"You see Marcia as young, Mother," said Ralph. "I wonder what she is to Hamish."

"Someone who can give him what he has not himself," said Simon. "It does not depend on youth."

"I feel I must say it, sir. I can't understand his turning to her after Naomi."

"It was because of the difference. They both had qualities on a large scale, of a high order, and not the same. The reason was there."

"I can't understand how you know so much about Marcia, when you have seen her so little."

"Understanding does not seem to be your strong point," said Simon, mildly. "I ought to know about her, and so ought we all. If we remember where we are, it is enough."

"It is too much," said Graham. "Our debt is too great. We are bowed down by it."

"I am not," said his father. "The change was not made in that spirit. A debt has to be repaid."

"It is a good photograph of her in your study, sir," said Ralph. "The one that was at first in the hall."

"Yes, I gave it a more intimate place," said Simon, in an open tone. "It seemed to deserve it of us. I could not feel at home myself in a public passage."

"It is strange how a photograph seems to hold something of the person it represents," said Julia.

"Simon made it sound as if it did," said Fanny.

"We don't usually have photographs about," said Ralph. "I thought we never did."

"Then I have done well by this one. I felt it had a claim. And it is only in my workroom, where it will not be seen."

"Or only by you," said Fanny.

"Well, a photograph is not meant to be seen by no one."

"I would not be without the photograph of my Hamish," said Julia. "It is what I have left of him. Or rather my memory is what I have left, and that is helped by it."

"Do we need help?" said Naomi. "No one who is dead can change. It is the living who grow different."

"So an early photograph may help us," said Simon. "We shall know what Marcia was like, when she came into our lives; and when she changed them."

"You ought to exhibit photographs of us all on that basis," said Ralph. "Those are things we all have done."

"You have, my boy. And the change goes on, and is with me. I do not need the photographs. I chose to pay this one a tribute."

"What made Marcia think of giving it to you? It is surely not a thing she does."

"She did not think of it. Father asked for it," murmured Naomi. "Will you ever stop pursuing the truth? Cannot you see it?"

"What will Hamish's children say to his giving up his heritage?" said Walter. "It is a question that must be asked. When they know about it, they may feel they are being sacrificed."

"Their mother will help both Hamish and them," said Simon.

"They may think it is you whom she has served," said Fanny.

"They will. They will know it. And that is not all they will learn. You are glad of the change, Fanny?"

176

"Yes, as you are, and in that measure. That is what makes the difference."

"I don't mind if we have no right to it," said Walter. "A thing seems to have more value, when it is not our due. But they may agree that it is not."

"Then they must learn the truth about Hamish and me," said Simon, quietly. "And know that he saw a father as coming before his son."

"But then they may feel that Hamish, as the elder son, should succeed you before Graham," said Ralph. "There may be troubles ahead."

"You sound as if you half-hoped there were," said Simon.

"Well, it seems rather empty without them. We have always had them smouldering underneath."

"It is I who have suffered them. You can neither need sympathy nor feel you do."

"I think I sometimes did. And ought troubles brought on ourselves to count as a claim for it?"

"No," said his father, gravely. "And they do not count. We deserve little pity for them, and have none."

"You have all mine," said his brother. "And I thought the troubles brought on ourselves were the worst?"

"The most disturbing," said Naomi. "But not the worst. We are not quite so careless of our own welfare."

"I should never bring troubles on myself," said Graham. "And I hardly think it is often done."

"It seems it ought to be," said Walter. "To leave them to come on other people, and be immune ourselves, seems so self-regarding."

"The immunity cannot be relied on," said Julia. "I have not been immune."

"Then of course it cannot," said her son; "or you would have been."

"Hamish is a person I never quite understand," said Graham.

"Do we understand anyone?" said Julia.

"Yes, many people fairly well, Grandma."

"You mean you think so."

"No, I mean what I said. That is what you mean."

"What is your trouble?" said his father.

"Well, he seems to do and think what I should not myself."

"Do not most people do that?"

"No, most people do just the same."

"Most people would have kept their inheritance," said Walter.

"Yes, and that is the same."

"But you like your new position, in spite of knowing that," said Ralph.

"I said I was the same as most people," said his brother.

"Hamish is easily influenced," said Fanny. "That is all it is."

"So it is well that he has come under the influence he has," said Simon. "And I do not mean what I can be taken to mean."

"No, I suppose not," said his wife, smiling. "You would hardly dare to mean it."

"It is good to be back in this house for the end of my life," said Julia. "I thought I had left it for ever. It seems to me now that I have hardly been away."

"It almost does to me," said Simon. "It is because our hearts were here."

"So Father's heart was not with us," said Ralph. "That seems to explain a good deal."

"What are you whispering?" said Simon. "I suppose you do not say it aloud, in case we should hear. Well, it may be a good reason."

"Was Father's personality here as well as his heart?" said Graham. "That was not with us, if this is what it is. No wonder he was glad to return, when so much of him was left behind. It must have been awkward to be without it."

"Well, we know it was," said Naomi.

"My Naomi is more herself," said Simon. "Our home gives its help to all of us."

"It must give the least to her," said Ralph.

"You cannot leave it unsaid? Ah, well, you have been through a disturbing time."

"I thought Father's personality was leaving us again for the moment," said Graham. "We are used to being without it, but where would it go? It would hardly pay a visit to the other house."

"It was never there," said Simon, as he overheard. "It never found it a home. It was something torn in two."

"It is strange that a house should absorb a human being," said Fanny. "I could have made my home under any roof."

"If I had not prevented it," said her husband. "But I could not see you or your children there. To me it was hardly a shelter for you."

"You saw it as the one we were to have. There was to be no other."

"I wonder if I did," said Simon, almost to himself. "Did something tell me that my place was here, that my service to it made it mine?"

"Not until Marcia told you. It is one of the things you learned from her."

"Walter, you are glad to be here again? It is your home as well as mine?"

"You know I grew up here with you."

"But I did not," said Fanny. "The house may be too much for me, as it was for my sister. And as it seems to be to my children."

"It will be other things," said Simon. "It is many more."

"What are they?" said Ralph. "I don't mean I do not see them. But I like to have things put into words."

"It is beautiful and complete in itself, and tells of a generous life lived in it for centuries."

"Lived by whom?" said Naomi.

"By a family who thought of the people about them, and strove to meet their needs."

"And looked for return in good measure. They arranged for the generous life. They must have approved of it."

"What do you say, Deakin?" said Walter. "You are the authority here."

"Well, there was dependence on the large house, sir, when there was such a thing. There was no call on people to be generous. And I would not have applied the term to many."

"And now they have what they need?"

"Yes, sir, and so the term is not in question."

"I am glad of that," said Walter. "I don't like to think of human generosity. I can imagine what a strain it would be. I have never had anything to spare, and it would be one then. But I fear I am a person who finds it difficult to give."

"You would not have given your mite, if you had been the widow?" said Graham.

"Not unless I had known the credit I should have. I think the mite did well for her. But I feel I should not have had it."

"Hamish has not had enough for what he has done," said Julia.

"If he had, we could not accept it," said Graham. "And he meant us to do that."

"Or Marcia did," said Fanny.

"Well, it was the same thing, Mother."

"Yes, it had come to be."

"Hamish likes to be led," said Walter. "I should like it myself, if anyone would lead me. We need not stress it too much."

"We are not doing so," said Fanny. "We are like you, and do not want to think of human generosity."

"He did not wish for credit," said Simon. "Should we have in his place?"

"We should not have been in it," said Naomi. "That shows how we should have wished for it."

"It would have been my reason for being in it," said Ralph.

"It was not his," said Simon.

"It seems odd that he should have the title and not the place. Not even Marcia can help that. And it will go to their descendants."

"Either his branch or mine will be without a son in the end. The two will be united. I have no fear."

"I suppose you would be glad, if he had no son?"

"I had not thought of it. I see it would simplify things."

"Would you like to be Sir Simon?"

"If it fell to me. But it will not. And enough has done so."

"Father's imagination has been at work," said Ralph to his sister.

"Well, why should it be idle? And it has not gone far beyond the truth."

"It has had no reason to. Mine would have been of little use, if it had done no more."

"Well, I daresay it has done you good, whatever it has done," said Simon. "I think being carried beyond ourselves carries ourselves further."

"This change that has come over Father! How far can we depend on it? Suppose we put it to the test and found it fail! I wonder he does not feel conscious about displaying it."

"He is too happy to care," said Naomi.

"And why should I disguise it?" said Simon. "I did not disguise my unhappiness. And one is as natural as the other. I have my home and my family, and little fault to find with either. And they fit each other, as I felt they would."

"We shall soon have to pay Father a return compliment," said Ralph. "I cannot be the one to do it. I have not his gift for carrying off a personal change. I cannot be his true son. Well, I have never thought I was. And neither has he."

"What are you saying about me?"

"That I am not your true son, sir."

"Well, all we have to do is to be ourselves."

"This above all——" said Julia. "And we know what follows."

"Is Father true to himself in this house or the other?" said Graham. "If in this one, it follows that in the other he was false to every man. Though perhaps less to the women."

"I find I almost like the falseness better," said Ralph. "So it is true that we can like people for their weaker side."

"You hardly seemed to," said Naomi. "And when we do that, it is generally their only side. This case is by itself."

"Well, I must be one of those people who love the old days. And I did not suspect it."

"You must remember that my youth in this house is the old time to me," said Simon.

"And to you mother, my son," said Julia. "You left your real self behind in it. I waited for it to return, for your children to see it, and could not have waited much longer. But when we found it here, waiting for us, I was not surprised. Your mother had understood."

"And not my wife?" said Simon.

"Well, you had to suffer the lot that carried your livelihood," said Fanny. "I could not see you as the martyr it seems you were. If that was failing as a wife, I failed. And if your attitude was failing as a husband, you failed also. Yes, what is it, Deakin?"

"A telegram, ma'am. It has come this moment. The boy is waiting."

Simon tore open the envelope and read the words.

"'Hamish ill with heart trouble. Very little hope. Marcia Challoner.'"

There was the silence, the grasp of the truth, the effort to rise to suspense. Julia was the first to speak.

"His mother is with him."

"And his wife," said Naomi.

"It is all he can have," said Simon, thinking, as he spoke, that his father was not, and seeing that others thought it.

"Ought we to go to them?" said Fanny. "Would they wish it?"

"We cannot know," said Graham. "And you might be too late. Other word will follow."

"I shall go," said Simon, moving to the door. "Whether I am in time or not, I can be of help. I will send the message."

Before it was time for him to leave, the second telegram came.

"Hamish died easily. No child coming. Marcia Challoner."

"I must go to my sister," said Fanny. "I will go with Simon."

"Yes, go, my dear," said Julia. "I will do what I can here."

There was another silence.

"So Hamish has left us," said Naomi. "Well, he had chosen to leave us. But this is not what he chose."

"How Marcia is what she is!" said Simon, almost to himself. "To tell the whole, so as to leave no doubt or question."

"And how Father is the same!" muttered Ralph. "Even at this moment I must say it."

"Why must you?" said Walter. "No one else has had to."

"The short, strange life!" said Fanny. "How much difference it brought, and how little it seems to leave! And how much will be left!"

"So the place and the title are united again," said Graham. "And does either seem to matter?"

"Neither does," said his father. "We are involved in things that do."

The talk went on, lifeless, unrelated to the depths, until Simon and Fanny left them. There was a feeling that anything more must wait until they had gone, that it might delay their going. Julia watched them go, and then turned to her grandchildren.

"I have lost a grandson. I must say it once. I would not, while your mother was with us. I would not say it to you, if there was anyone else to hear. I know you have not lost a brother. But let me say once that I have thought of Hamish as what he is—what he was to me, and wished he could know I thought it. I wish I had told him. To live is nothing but wishing. It is always too late."

"I don't see how you could tell him," said Graham. "It was what was not to be told. But for that reason he may have known."

"So he is dead," said Julia. "The boy who made so much trouble, brought so much change, whose nature had to be forgotten. It is over, what should not have been, what will never be as if it had not been. It is in the past."

The words were true, and the past fell into its place. Things moved in the accustomed way and became a part of it. Simon returned for Hamish's burial in the family vault, and with his sons followed him to it. Fanny came home later, leaving Hamish's mother with his wife. The day came when the family gathered at the table, feeling they had reached a settled stage in their lives.

"So there can be no more change," said Julia, "until one of us follows Hamish. I shall be the first."

"It is a high destiny, Mater," said Walter. "But do you sound as if your heart was in it?"

"I have dear ones here and dear ones there. This has added another to them. And there the truth will have its place. Nothing will have to be hidden."

"Nothing should need to be," said Graham. "Or the sphere you mean would hardly exist."

"These are not matters for jest," said Simon. "They are real to some of us. That should be enough. And perhaps it is hardly a time for jest at all."

"Any time is good for that," said Fanny. "A jest need be no more than it is."

"Well, let it be the time. But let some subjects be forbidden."

"So Marcia and Aunt Rhoda are to live together, like the pair in the Bible," said Ralph.

"Yes," said his father, without looking at him. "I have heard from Marcia. They are soon to return home. They will not remain in the other place without Hamish. And your aunt must be near your mother. They are thinking of the house by the river, where the roads meet. Our other house is too large for them."

"Marcia is a Ruth indeed," said Fanny. "Where Rhoda dwelleth she will dwell. Her people will be her people, and I daresay her God would be her God, if she felt there could be one."

"Fanny, that is hardly talk for you," said Simon. "And you will be glad to have your sister, and help her as you can. You know you felt her going."

"She will have my help, if she needs it. She has always done so. This other dependence is a new one."

"Such things are not a matter of time. Friendships are made in a moment; marriages are made. A feeling that will last a lifetime, may spring into being. We all know cases of it."

"I do not. Tell me of one."

"There is my feeling for you," said Simon, smiling. "We were old friends when we married; but there was a time when there was a movement of one to the other. There must have been."

"Well, then we can say there was."

"There will be things to arrange, sir," said Graham. "Death duties will have to be met. And there will be another widow."

"Hamish made everything over to me but a small competence. The duty that Marcia will pay, will not be large. That on Hamish's inheritance from his father has been decided. We are not the better for it, but with care we shall recover."

185

"It is time that I died and made a widow less," said Julia.

"And that many of us did, if the object is to save our expenses," said Walter. "Mine are too small for it to be worth while. It will never be my time."

"Either as a man or a poet," said Ralph. "You should be doubly immortal."

"Shall we ever learn that people's life ambitions are not humorous to them?" said Naomi.

"They ought to be," said Walter. "We are forbidden to take ourselves seriously."

"But who else would do so?" said Graham. "And what would happen, if no one did?"

"Nothing does happen," said Walter.

The door opened and Claud and Emma entered, bearing a garland between them.

"It is to celebrate things being usual again," said Claud, putting it over his mother's chair. "But we made it like a wreath, because of Hamish. And we like this house, now we are used to it. Of course it was a change for us to go up in the world."

"How have you done that?" said Julia.

"Just by belonging to the family," said Emma, lifting her brows. "We rise and fall together."

"You can think of Hamish living in this house, when he was as young as you are."

"Yes, we do; we shall always remember him. Of course he might have been our brother. I think some people say he was. But they must mean he would have been, if he had married Naomi."

"It gives us a feeling for him," said Claud. "But it is not our fault that he is dead. Perhaps Marcia did not keep an eye on him. Emma hardly dares to take hers off me."

"He will always be a charge," said Emma, with a sigh.

"We have not thanked you for the wreath," said Fanny. "It is a very pretty one."

"It is a simple offering," said Claud. "But simple things are as good as any others."

"It places people, if they don't think so," said Emma.

"How are you doing with your lessons?" said Simon, reminded of these by the signs of advance. "Is Miss Dolton pleased with you?"

"Yes, I can read as well as Emma now. And she can almost read handwriting. Here is something she has read."

"'Dear Simon,'" read Emma, opening a letter, "'The bond between us is broken, but we have our own. And our lives will move on side by side. We shall have help as we need it. There must be something to give——'"

"You must not read letters," said Simon, taking it from her. "Where did you get this one?"

"It was on the floor in the hall. Someone must have dropped it. We have to read writing when we can, to get some practice. Or we shan't be able to read it, when we are grown-up."

"And it will be no good for people to write to us," said Claud.

"Well, it does not matter, as it happens. It is one of those letters without much meaning."

"It might have a hidden one. But 'Marcia' is the name at the end. And she is our relation. So it couldn't be much."

"She is still our cousin by marriage," said Claud, "even though Hamish is dead. And she is your cousin as well."

"A nearer one than to us," said Emma. "I don't think you could marry her, if Mother died. Though she might be the person you would think of."

"Now your tongues are running away with you," said Simon. "It is the work your legs ought to be doing. So let us see them do it."

The children broke into mirth, glanced down at the limbs in question, and ran away to repeat the words.

"You must be glad of the friendship between Marcia and your sister, Fanny," said Julia at once. "It will be an answer to many problems."

"Her feelings and mine do seem to have followed similar lines."

"Well, I must go to my work in the garden. I want help for a little while. Are my grandchildren coming to give it to me?"

"While we are on such matters, ma'am," said Deakin, "is the creeper on the house to be cut back? Sir Simon dislikes it to encroach."

"We will give it a respite, Deakin," said Simon. "Encroachment seems to be its work. And we are so inured to the shadow, that we might be startled by the light."

"Well, other light is thrown, ma'am," said Deakin, smiling at Julia, as he left them.

"Fanny," said Simon, when the others had gone, "you do not read more into that letter than was there?"

"I see how it was meant to be read."

"We must help people in trouble as we can."

"And it is good to help those who help themselves. But when Marcia was here, she was not in trouble."

"She knew her real relation to me. That justifies anything that needs it."

"Suppose something in my life did that! It would be a change. And you would find it so."

"Fanny, I admire and envy you, that nothing in your life has needed excuse or ever will."

"It is true of me, too," said Walter. "Or has been since my getting into debt at Cambridge. And that had it, as my allowance was too small."

"Walter, you and I have seen and done much together."

"Well, Walter has seen it," said Fanny. "And it has been a good deal."

"Claud and Emma are more natural with me than the elder children were."

"Well, what are you with them? You must see the reason."

"I ought not to have let my personal trouble harm me as it did."

"Well, you have allowed the ending of it to restore you.

188

It is an honest confession that your character depends on your own content."

"I could take a lesson from my Naomi there," said Simon, looking out of the window at his children returning to the house. "I hope her brothers will do for her what mine has for me. They have taken that room off the hall for their sanctum. May they have many happy hours in it."

"Let us have one now," said Ralph, as they passed. "It is good to have a place where we can be by ourselves, in other words without Father. His new personality makes me ill at ease. Or I suppose it is his old one. I am the more disturbed, that I have had no part in our recent history. My life is untouched, and yet the workhouse has disappeared from it. And I suppose its descendant, the orphanage, has done the same. It shows how far they were the figment of Father's brain."

"People are supposed to love their own creations," said Naomi. "It is disloyal of Father to be so unfaithful to his."

"Unfaithful to what?" said Simon, in the doorway. "It sounds a grave charge. So this is your sanctum, your refuge from storm and stress. To what am I unfaithful?"

"To your conception of the future, sir," said Ralph. "The workhouse has been banished. And in the case of some of us without any ground."

"The reason is here," said Simon, looking about him. "This is your background, your refuge in case of need. I had to think of you without them. Now your brother will be behind you. My death would not leave you destitute. I can live my own life at ease about yours. No one gives up the idea of the workhouse more willingly. No one else knows how real to me it was. Well, it cast the lesser shadow. I am glad the cloud was mine."

"Is Father a noble man?" said Ralph, as the door closed. "Or is he a deceiver of himself and others? Or what is he?"

"A mixture of them all, as we all are," said Naomi. "But exile exposed and stressed the parts. Suppose we had a similar love for our first home, and were affected by leaving it in the same way! He would hardly be able to complain. He may have been wise to darken our memories of it."

"I still fear a reaction from the new spirit. His position will become normal to him. It was indeed the other that was not. And he will have nothing besides."

"So that is what you think," said Graham.

"Well, thinking needs so much courage."

"I have enough," said Naomi. "The something besides will be there. And I am glad it will. It is not good to live without it."

"He is putting a memorial tablet to Hamish in the church," said Graham. "Hamish is to be described as Uncle Edwin's son. I daresay many people are not what they are thought to be."

"Most of them what they are known to be," said Naomi. "Secrets are not often kept. If they were, we should not know there were such things. And now we take more interest in them than in any others."

"As people may in this one," said Ralph. "And very likely do."

"The heroine of our whole story is Mother," said Graham.

"And who is the hero?" said Naomi.

"Hamish?" said her brother, in question.

"Uncle Walter might turn out to have been so all the time. But he is inclined to suggest it himself, and that is against it."

"Father," said Ralph. "It can be no one else. And if we think, it is no one else. Unless my saying it makes me the hero myself."